The Misted Mirror

Mindfulness for Schools and Universities

Dr Peter Mack

MBBS, FRCS, PhD, MBA, MHlthEcon, MMEd

Publication by *From the Heart Press*:
First Publication: July 2020
Website: www.fromtheheartpress.com

ISBN: 978-1-9999232-6-6

A CIP catalogue record of this book is available from the British Library.

Cover Design:
Ashleigh Hanson
Email: ash@shifted.co.nz

To contact the author:
Email: dr.pmack@gmail.com
Website: http://www.petermack.sg

Disclaimer

The information and stories provided in this book are designed to provide helpful information on mindfulness and to share the author's experience. There is no religious content. The ideas and advice provided are intended to promote awareness and not intended as a substitute for intervention by a qualified mental health professional. The names and identities of the people in the stories in this book have been disguised to protect confidentiality while preserving the spirit of the work. No claims are made of any miraculous effectiveness of the modality of mindfulness.

Acknowledgments

The free verses in the book are contributed by Ms Chong Jia Yi, a special-needs teacher, and are invaluable in enhancing the messages and themes in the book. Ms Michelle Loh and Dr Carol Loi have provided ideas for improvement of the main text of the book, while Ms Melody Wu, a college teacher, and Ms Dian Handayani, an art therapist, have contributed to the mindfulness-based art exercises in the Appendix. I am grateful to all the others who have contributed their personal experience of mindfulness and stories of their meditation retreats.

Testimonials

"This book adopts a holistic approach in the cultivation of mindfulness and its application to education. The author is very skilled in guiding the readers to navigate and experience what meditation is about, to establish the composure needed to connect with the inner self and acquire the wisdom to abandon the bad habits."

– Michelle Loh, lawyer

"This is a must-read book for anyone considering mindfulness practice. There isn't another book that could imbue our minds so well with compassion and peaceful tranquillity. It is an excellent guide to strengthen our mind to manage negative thoughts."

– Dr Carol Loi, genetic counsellor

"Written at a time of the global COVID-19 crisis when many young, vulnerable people are facing their first life-changing experience, this book is a valuable resource."

- Dr Chay Oh Moh, paediatrician

Contents

Preface

The school is a learning environment, and so is life as a whole. We are all on a learning journey in life, and schooling is but one phase of this journey, and a particularly important one. So, as we look mindfully at both the microcosmic and macrocosmic view of life, how then do we fit ourselves into our learning mission? This book is written for secondary and university students and their teachers. It is the goal of this book to address the issue of how mindfulness fulfils our mission in education.

When I received a request to write this book, it struck me that our societal and educational changes have gathered significant momentum in recent years. For some time, I have been reflecting on an appropriate way to deliver my message on mindfulness to educators and learners. I personally see mindfulness practice as analogous to going to a mental gym where we can build up the muscles of the mind. Mental gymnastics in turn will strengthen us both emotionally and socially.

Many mindfulness books have been written in recent years. Most of them are scripted from the perspective of stress and anxiety reduction, anger management, mental health and spiritual growth. In line with this, many people have perceived mindfulness as being reserved for the mentally vulnerable or spiritually profound. Far fewer people are aware of how it can benefit school children and teachers in terms of enhancing the learning process.

A colleague of mine was once perplexed as to why mindfulness would benefit not just learners but also teachers. I personally take the view that mindfulness is a wholesome act. While helping adolescents to learn and develop into wholesome adults in a rapidly changing world, it also helps our educationists to shape the curriculum and school environment towards a path of holistic education.

I recall giving a talk to a group of school counsellors some years ago and noticed something unique. I gathered that their interest in mindfulness was rooted in their intent to promote resilience in school children. This was related to and triggered by the fact that our local suicide rates of school children were rising over the years. For that reason, I have included a discussion of the application of mindfulness to cultivating resilience in this book.

There is a subtle amount of profoundness in the philosophical underpinnings of the mindfulness concept. To facilitate acceptance, I have attempted to structure the concept and practice from a rational standpoint so that students can better relate with it. I hope by doing so, it will help them to intellectually grasp the essence of how the training of our attentiveness in the classroom is achievable through a simple, non-threatening process.

In the spirit of simplicity, mindfulness is being expressed as a way of the person being aware of what is happening to or around him at a particular moment. This helps the student to understand his need to cultivate a habitual discipline of pausing from time to time to take notice of his learning situation. In taking a step back from the fast pace of schoolroom activities, he would then learn to put his mental chatter to the background and make space for optimising his learning ability.

I have refrained from including the results of neuroscientific research on the benefits of mindfulness in this book. The goal of this book is not to provide evidence of the benefits but to guide readers on how to make the most of the discipline and techniques to enrich their educational process. For those without a background knowledge of human brain structure and function, findings in neurophysiological research is likely to appear too complex and overwhelming. Rather, I have chosen to focus on the use of mindfulness in retraining the student's mind, and in unleashing the learning power within. The core purpose is to help students to process their lives as successful adults.

I will present some historical background to encourage the reader to reflect on the evolution of the notion of mindfulness over the past three thousand years. Equally appealing is perhaps the impact of mindfulness on educational psychology. Through this perspective, educators and educationists may be excited to link and interlace the philosophy of mindfulness with principles of holistic learning and living.

On a stylistic note, when referring to students in general I have tended to use masculine pronouns throughout rather than what can be the somewhat stilted he/she and so on. This is purely to help the flow of the text; the techniques explained in this book naturally apply equally to male and female students.

Dr Peter Mack
Singapore

The Mist

Breezes of cold air blowing,
Into the room,
Onto your skin,
Into your heart,
The chills that reached in for you,
Trying to get a hold of you,
You let it wash over you.

You trembled spreading from your core outwards,
The sight of the heavy drizzle,
The grey sky of thick cold fog,
The buildings are covered in the thick cold fog,
Somehow it looks familiar,
It's how your heart looks like,
Foggy, misty, unclear.

With a heavy drape,
Of thick cold fog around it,
Wait for the rain to stop,
Wait for the fog to disperse,
Till then your heart will be clear,
Strong and whole again,
Be still.

By: Chong Jia Yi

Chapter One

Quieting the Mind

Mindfulness refers to a person's tendency to remain attentive to his own experience, thoughts and feelings in a non-judgmental manner. It is a wonderful technique that all of us can use to master and restore the tranquillity in ourselves. This is because it helps us to attain a state where we feel totally unattached to anything in the world and without inclination to cling on to anything. When we attain this mental state, we find it easier to see things and situations below the superficial level of opinions. This is a time-honoured approach and has been well accepted as a means to improve wellness and provide us with a sense of fulfilment. However, there is also a growing body of evidence showing that mindfulness also has substantial benefits for teachers and students in the school environment.

The Quiet Mind in Education

There are four main areas in which mindfulness is relevant to the student. First and foremost, it helps him to manage stress. Failing to answer a question when called in front of an entire class is usually stressful. So is forgetting his homework or not meeting parents' expectations in exam scores. In calming the mind with the help of mindfulness, the student can reduce the negative effects of stress and help himself to stay on track academically. Calmness helps to reduce the student's emotional reactivity so that there are fewer obstacles getting in the way of learning.

Secondly, mindfulness helps to improve attentiveness, which is of paramount importance in the classroom environment. Enhanced attention means that the student will be able to take in more information without being distracted by his own reaction or preconceived ideas.

Thirdly, mindfulness improves working memory and cognitive reasoning, especially in studies. Regular meditation practice is known to increase blood flow to the brain, leading to a stronger network of blood vessels being built in the brain cortex, reinforcing memory capacity and cognitive functioning. This would in turn impact positively on the goal-directed behaviour of the student in the acquisition of new knowledge.

The fourth benefit, and one that is often overlooked, is the cultivation of an innovative and creative mind. Each of us, as a learner, has an enormous amount of curiosity and imagination which, when activated, can unleash our creativity within and transform our ability in problem-solving.

While it is easy to understand why schools need the mindfulness discipline to boost the learning capacity of students, we may be wondering if mindfulness is also important for teachers. Personally, I believe the answer is an undeniable *yes.* The underlying reason is simple: mindful teachers are master teachers.

Mindful teachers are aware of themselves and attuned to their students. For them, there is a conscious and purposeful tuning in to what is happening in and around the classroom environment. They understand their own emotions better. They relate with their students better and understand the problems underlying the behaviour of those students who are disruptive in class. They are also more aware of how to set up a positive learning environment for their students. The ability to improve mental focus through mindfulness is therefore important for the academic performance of both teachers and students alike.

Mental Stillness

Many of us might think that the mind is something that belongs to ourselves. For this reason, we tend to believe that we are in firm control of our own thought processes. In reality, this is seldom the case. Rather, we tend to allow most of our daily lives to be governed by our routines. This is often permitted in the hope of freeing our mind for things that we consider more useful. Unfortunately, our mind on its own tends to choose to produce a constant whirlpool of thoughts, remarks and judgments. This whirlpool generates a combination of mental words and images that pull us away from our true selves. We generally remain unaware of this fact and, as a result, we continue to entertain thoughts that serve no value in our lives.

> *"The equivalent of external noise is the inner noise of thinking. The equivalent of external silence is inner stillness."*
>
> *- Eckhart Tolle*

Often, in getting along with our lives, we compare ourselves with others. We feel upset when we fail to match up to their performances or to our own expectations. Such judgments on ourselves and others are usually based on trivial evidence. We start to spin stories about ourselves that we believe might be true. Then we find ourselves unable to turn our thoughts and judgments around, nor able to make them do what we want. This *Story of Self* affects our moods, studies and daily work. More so, it influences our morale, decision-making process and our relationships in our daily lives.

Interestingly, when we look back on how we inadvertently created such mental states, we notice that the focus of most of these thoughts resides with unhappy events from our past, including unpleasant childhood memories. Sometimes they are based on our dreams or desires for the future. Hardly ever are these thoughts and judgments focused on the *present.* Herein lies the importance of emphasising the present moment and the value of mindfulness.

Mindfulness is currently being taught as a practice of developing an orientation to the *present moment.* There is ample evidence to conclude that its cultivation facilitates adaptive psychological functioning, which in turn increases our wellbeing.[1]

In this book, the reader will learn to perceive the mind as a tool that he can use to cultivate inner calm, attentiveness and clarity of mental focus. He will be able to use it to improve his studies, but he can also use it for nurturing resilience in his journey of growth and maturity. In particular, he will see the relevance of mindfulness in stressful situations commonly faced by many of us in our current, fast-paced education system.

Ways of Understanding Mindfulness

Mindfulness is a multifaceted concept and it can be viewed from different perspectives. Commonly, the term is understood from three angles: firstly, as a *mental construct* of attaining moment-by-moment awareness; secondly, as a *physiological process* of being mindfully aware of our environment; and thirdly, as a *practice* of cultivating a state of awareness and attention through a meditative approach.

---

[1] Keng, S.L. et al., "Effects of Mindfulness on Psychological Health: A

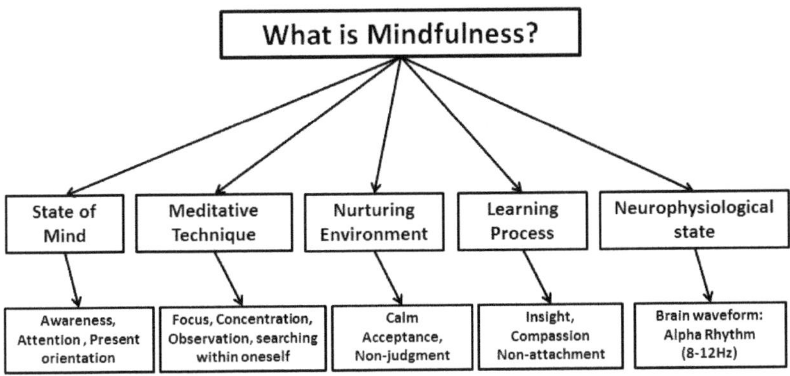

In recent years, mindfulness practice has gained momentum in both Eastern and Western cultures. Its emphasis on the cultivation of self-awareness has seen it increasingly being accepted and adopted by the healthcare community for the promotion of wellness and for psychotherapy. Subsequently, the basic concepts of *awareness and attention* in mindfulness have been duly expanded by psychotherapists to include the qualities of *neutrality, non-judgment* and *acceptance.* These qualities are to be developed by the individual who is engaged in cultivating mindfulness as part of his healing journey. Yet, from the educational perspective, these qualities are equally pertinent for teachers who wish to improve teaching skills and for students who need to cope with the challenges in their learning environment.

From the background of educational psychology, mindfulness can be looked at from five perspectives.

Mindfulness as a Mental State

As a mental state, mindfulness has three main elements: *awareness, concentration* and *one-pointedness.* These elements are essential in the focusing of our experience from moment to moment. They are effective not only as tools for learning but also function as antidotes to common forms of psychological stress, including anxiety, frustration, fear, anger and depression.

In its simplest form, mindfulness can be considered a state of focused attention with total non-attachment. In other words, it involves an absence of desire of the individual to cling on to anything in the world. In the process, the person attains a moment-by-moment awareness of himself and the world around him. Eventually he is able to reach a state of mental profoundness in which he sees things deep down and beyond the intellectual level of concepts and opinions.

Focused concentration is fundamental to the classroom environment. When we are focused, our mental state can clear up our delusions and we become mentally brighter. Once our mind is clear, we can direct our concentration to penetrate within to a deeper level to develop insight into not only the subject matter of what we are learning, but into ourselves as well. Such a perception gives the student a sense of certainty of the content being learned and with complete absence of confusion. The profound awareness will manifest as a constant, unwavering attention and will neutralise the defilements in the mind. By defilement, I am referring to the state of pollution of thoughts, where a mind is clouded with pollutants such as anxiety, fear, anger, jealousy and desire. The result is that the student will be able to nurture a mental state that is unperturbed by the ups and downs of his journey of educational struggle. School is often turbulent these days. With the acquisition of penetrative insight, the mind is able to take the student a step further, from the acquisition of knowledge to the development of wisdom.

Mindfulness as Meditation

Learning to meditate is the greatest gift we can give ourselves in this life. More often than not, we overlook this natural gift and allow our lives to go to waste. For this reason we are often removed from our true selves.

We live our early life in an anxious struggle to compete, achieve and excel in our school performance. This often leads to an imbalance between the body and the mind, resulting in misery and sickness. To lead a balanced life, it is important that we retrain our mind to understand its true nature. This is best done through mindfulness meditation.

The term *meditation* refers to the deliberate practice of stilling the mind. The purpose is to acquire awareness of unperceived realities. By pursuing this awareness intelligently, it will lead us to a contemplative state and, thereafter, to an experience of reality. Meditation is not a mysterious technique that we learn to do. Rather, it is an inner experience that we learn to identify within ourselves. The process requires us to learn to recognise this experience and consciously connect with something that is already a real aspect of ourselves. While this statement may sound profound, the student who starts practising it will find that this experience is readily accessible.

The way that mindfulness meditation works is that it gives us a complete break from our normal life of stress. It helps us to free ourselves from unwanted concerns and desires. A desire is a wish or longing for something. It may be a longing for companionship, to influence other people, to be included in a school group or to get even with someone who has done us injustice. Desires determine our basic behaviour and unwanted desires create emotional stress in our lives. With meditative practice, we learn to stay neutral with our emotions and learn not to react to them.

In freeing ourselves from unwanted concerns, I am not referring to a purposeful rejection of life situations. The mindful individual is not running away from the realities of life through meditation. He is not being encouraged to deny truths. He is simply learning, through the meditative process, to slowly release the notions that have imprisoned him within a space of natural simplification. The purpose of meditation is to awaken in him the hidden power to realise what and who he truly is. In the stillness of the mind, he catches a glimpse of his authentic self and returns to his inner nature where many possibilities exist.

> *"Life is a mystery – mystery of beauty, bliss and divinity. Meditation is the art of unfolding that mystery."*
>
> *– Amit Ray*

Connecting with oneself is a creative experience. It is an inner undertaking that calls for concentration. It involves a deliberate search for an inner experience that underlies the constantly busy state of the brain. Through this undertaking, we seek to experience the ultimate fulfilment beyond the thought of who we are and what is in our deepest nature. People who meditate regularly and successfully will come to a state of contemplation in a way customised to their own temperament and personal store of information.

Mindfulness meditation is learned through regular and persistent practice. It has to be experienced and cannot be acquired through reading or attending talks. The essence of the mindfulness technique is *participatory observation*. The mindful practitioner is both a participant and an observer in the process. While he watches his own emotions and physical sensations in the meditative state, he is also feeling them at that very same moment. The awareness of his emotions and sensations is neither intellectual nor conceptual. It does not get involved with logic. The practitioner does not get hung up on ideas, opinions or past memories of the emotions. He just watches and observes them as if they are occurring for the first time.

In mindfulness, we do not compare the nature of different meditative experiences. Nor do we label or categorise them. The meditative discipline trains the individual to stay with his awareness of the present moment. Everything takes place in the here and now. The person observes what is happening in the present without reference to self. He also does not make reference to the observed experiences as belonging to him. He watches these experiences go by, says "hello" to them and regards them as a passing flow.

> *"When meditation is mastered, the mind is unwavering like the flame of a candle in a windless place."*
>
> *- Bhagavad Gita*

As the individual becomes more aware of the constant flux of experiences and events, he improves his understanding of the process of change. He learns to see the genesis, growth and decay of all phenomena in life. As he continues to practise, he learns to see and realise how those phenomena could impact on his emotional self. He understands how he might have reacted to them if he was not aware. This involves the qualities of *non-judgment* and *acceptance*. The person must have the correct attitude and learn to stay neutral to what he realises or observes. He must also learn to apply the correct amount of energy needed to do the job. When this energy is applied appropriately, he will find himself staying constantly in a state of calm and alertness.

From this description we can see that our current model of mindfulness includes two main elements: (a) a self-regulation of *focused attention* with (b) an element of *monitoring*.

In *focused attention*, the awareness of our sensations, thoughts or feelings from moment-to-moment is made possible by anchoring our attention to a single object.

The object can be our breath, a part of the body or a visual image of an external article. A more detailed explanation of meditation objects will be given in the next chapter. Nurturing ourselves on the focused attention will lead us on to the second element of *open monitoring*.

Mindfulness as Nurturing and Change

The open monitoring in mindfulness is involved with the adoption of a particular orientation or attitude towards our experiences during the meditation process. Instead of focusing on any one particular object, we keep our attention open and monitor all aspects of our meditative experience. This includes all body sensations and feelings that may arise during the process. If necessary, we may scan the body to locate them. The required attitude is one of *openness* and *acceptance*.

Let us not be mistaken, however. In being open to and accepting the experience, we are neither resigned to fate nor learning to be passive to the experience. Rather, we experience the events during our meditation fully and neutrally, without reacting to or suppressing them. This requires us to refrain from judging the nature of those meditative experiences, be they pleasant or painful.

Non-judgment is important in fostering mindfulness, especially when we are dealing with difficult emotional states. An aspiring school student whose exam scores fall below the required standard for getting into university is often emotionally shocked. But, by not judging his experience, he is more likely to be able to see the situation as it is without getting overly upset or disturbed.

Acceptance, on the other hand, is an act of favourable reception and represents an extension of the concept of non-judgment. It adds on a sense of approval and positive outlook with an added measure of self-kindness.

Acceptance means the student is willing to let things be as they are, the moment he becomes aware of what has happened. Likewise, any other past experiences that may arise during meditation, be they pleasant or painful, are accepted as they arise.

When a student is working through difficult emotions, be it shame, anger, fear or guilt, it is equally important for the mindful teacher to maintain an open, compassionate and accepting attitude. Empathy and positive regard are important relational aspects that overlap with acceptance. These behavioural qualities are important for nurturance and change in the school environment.

> *"A man must find time for himself. Time is what we spend our lives with. If we are not careful, we find others spending it for us ... It is necessary now and then for a man to go away by himself and experience loneliness; to sit on a rock in the forest and to ask of himself, 'Who am I, and where have I been, and where am I going?' ... If one is not careful, one allows diversions to take up one's time – the stuff of life."*
>
> *– Carl Sandburg*

In coping with intensive daily study schedules, the student needs quiet time to ponder and reflect, and sees this as part of a change process. This reflective process is called *contemplation.* In mindfulness, contemplative silence is the door that provides access to the space for the student to open up possibilities for change. The change involved is often of a slow and steady nature, but it can sometimes take the form of an epiphany.[2]

Paradoxically, in integrating ourselves into today's busy world, many of us do think and behave differently.

---

[2] An epiphany is a sudden perception of the essential nature or meaning of something. To the individual it feels like an intuitive grasp or an illuminating discovery.

"Do we really need quiet time? Shouldn't we train ourselves to adapt to all kinds of environment and execute multiple tasks simultaneously?" I would say that the answer is a definite *no*. When faced with demanding situations, we need to choose effectiveness over efficiency; multi-tasking is an ineffective way to achieve the outcomes that we want.

The concept of multi-tasking has its origin in computer technology during the era of the 1960s. It was used to describe the function of the computer in the concurrent execution of multiple processes over a period of time. Since then, many people have proposed that human beings could do likewise to achieve greater efficiency. Today, multi-tasking is being widely promoted as a great way to get a lot of things done at once. The truth is that research has shown this approach to reduce human productivity.

In human multi-tasking, what we are really doing is quickly shifting our attention and focus from one task to the next. This act of constant switching makes it difficult for us to filter out distractions. Instead, it encourages mental blocks that slow down our performance. With insufficient attention, multi-tasking tends to cause more errors. It is categorically not the recommended solution for students in a stressful classroom environment and is to be strongly discouraged.

The *noise-to-signal* analogy as taught in our Physics lessons is an excellent way to help us to appreciate the nature of mindfulness. All electronic audio-devices, be it the radio, telephone or television, create some level of background noise in addition to the main audio signal. For the audio signal to be heard clearly and distinctly, it is essential to keep the background noise level sufficiently low. In a similar manner, there is a constant chatter that goes on in our mind all the time. Some people like to call this the *monkey mind.*[3] In limiting this mental chatter, it is essential to develop a mental state that is of a low-enough *noise level* to tell whether the *signal* that we receive has something meaningful to tell us, or whether it is part of the noise background. Mindfulness meditation is the tool that helps us to achieve this end. It reduces the noise-to-signal level in our mind and provides us with the needed clarity.

We can take an example in nature to further illustrate this. When we drop a pebble into a pond with calm water, noticeable ripples show up. Concentric circles of waveforms are generated and continually increase in diameter. The circles widen before their peripheral circumferences fade off into the boundaries of the pond. We can see the fine movements of this spreading waveform clearly on the water surface and gradually fading off at the pond edges. Imagine that a thunderstorm comes next, and we find the situation distinctly different. The ripples created by the impact of the same pebble on the turbulent water surface will no longer be detectable. The turbulence created by the storm has masked all the signals from the pebble.

Mindfulness can also be understood as an awareness of change. When we observe the fading circles of ripples on the pond, it is like observing the passing flow of experience. It is a process of watching things as they are changing. In mindfulness practice, we look at the genesis, growth and decay of all phenomena in our lives. We watch them come and go away. It is seeing how those phenomena make us feel and react to them. It recollects awareness into the present, helps us to remember ourselves and ensures that our actions are purposeful, appropriate and grounded in time and place. Mindfulness

---

[3] The term *monkey mind* has a Sino-Japanese origin (心猿), literally meaning heart-mind monkey.

guards our senses. It endows us with circumspection and restrains our senses to modify our desires.

Taking the concept forward, we can see mindfulness as being more than just mental concentration. Mere concentration entails a restriction of attention to a single object, leading to a withdrawal of sensory and other inputs. In contrast, mindfulness involves a fluid regulation of states of attention and awareness. It has flexibility. We can focus on multiple objects and changing states. The flexibility can move us back from particular states of mind to gain a larger perspective on what is taking place. It also allows us to zero in on situational details.

Mindfulness as a Way of Learning about Life

Mindfulness meditation is not easy. We have to set aside time and make effort to practise it regularly as a discipline. It is far easier for the student after school to sit back and watch television as a mode of relaxation. Why then should we recommend mindfulness when there are other enjoyable ways to unwind? Again, the answer is simple. It is because we are human.

> *"Meditation practice isn't about trying to throw ourselves away and become something better. It's about befriending who we are already."*
>
> *– Pema Chödrön*

As a human being, there is an inherent feeling of dissatisfaction in our lives. We have all experienced this feeling at some time and find that it will not go away, no matter how we unwind. There is always a feeling of a need or yearning to have more of something, but not knowing what it is. There is often a strong desire to perform better in a subject area in which we are already making progress. Unconsciously, we often deny this feeling, suppress it or even hide away from it. However, we find that we often tend to get stuck with dreams of our desires. We tell ourselves: "If only I could score higher in my mid-year exam, I would be satisfied." "If only my parents had had more time for me when I was a child, I would be a happier adult." "If only I'd had more pocket money, my school days would have been more enjoyable." The list goes on. With all these desires, life seems like a constant struggle for all of us, so long as we are human.

A generation ago, children in schools spent much of their time playing, drawing or creating imaginary worlds in their mind. However, in today's environment where the emphasis is on teacher-led didactic instruction, formal education starts very early, even at kindergarten and pre-school. The thinking is that without this early start, children will fall behind in crucial subjects such as language and maths and may never catch up. The idea that *starting sooner means learning more* has become prevalent in many societies, especially in Asian countries. Play is perceived as immature behaviour that does not help to achieve anything. This approach has unfortunately led to much dissatisfaction and disappointment. Studies have shown that children who received more didactic instruction tend to have significantly lower grades than those who had been allowed more opportunities to learn through play.

By the time we reach teenage, we learn to manage our disappointments typically by distraction. We hang out in fast-food outlets, watch movies, play computer games and check smartphones. However, the sense of dissatisfaction will always come back. We have set the never-good-enough criteria for judging our performance. We may also have learned the belief somewhere that unrealistic standards and harshness on ourselves are the only paths to motivation and achieving success. Then, out of the blue, we may one day realise the exact situation in our life that we are unhappy about.

With mindfulness practice, we learn to watch our inner universe. We begin to study our experience, thoughts, feelings and perceptions and become less concerned with the external environment. The universe within us has a rich store of information. Studying this information enables us to acquire mental freedom. We suddenly realise that there is a whole realm of new understanding of the richness of life and clarity that we have not been aware of. When this realisation comes about, it makes our bad times fade away.

> *"Peace is the result of retraining your mind to process life as it is, rather than as you think it should be."*
>
> *– Wayne W. Dyer*

In the course of my career, many patients have sought help for their emotional problems in addition to their physical diseases. Among them, a few have undergone a major change in their lives through mindfulness meditation. One of them has even terminated his business and turned himself into a mindfulness teacher. However, for a transformational change to take place, we need to integrate the mindfulness practice into our lives. Otherwise, it may just be reduced into a stress-relieving exercise that we do for a short period of time each day. A short-term approach will contribute to only minor changes in our lives.

For a major change, the personal work doesn't stop with just meditation. Instead, the daily routine will include a practice of conscious living with constant awareness and choice of wise action. We name this practice as *everyday mindfulness*. It involves us being mindful of whatever action we undertake, be it eating, walking, studying or driving. A narrative illustration of the practice of everyday mindfulness, in the context of contemplative learning, is presented in Chapter 5.

Mindfulness as a Neurophysiological State

Perhaps the science student may find it more appealing to understand the mindful state in quantifiable terms as defined by electrical brain activity. In all of us, brain waves are produced by synchronised electrical pulses from groups of nerve cells, called *neurons*. These neurons connect and communicate with each other within the brain substance. In fact, this inter-neuron communication lies at the core of all our thoughts and emotions, and the brain waveforms vary instantly with fluctuations in our emotional state.

Brain waves were first recorded by Hans Berger,[4] who invented the EEG (electroencephalogram) in 1924. The EEG is a non-invasive, electro-physiological method of monitoring brain activity, using electrodes placed on designated positions on the scalp. With the advance of computer technology, the electrical waveforms of the brain can be easily analysed mathematically through Fourier Transform and Wavelet Analysis nowadays. These waveforms are then broken down into different components and displayed as waves of different bandwidths on separate channels on the computer screen. Depending on their frequencies, they are named as beta (12–30 Hz), alpha (8–12 Hz), theta (4–8 Hz) and delta (0.5–4.0 Hz) waves. These categories of waveforms have been found to correspond closely to various conscious states of the brain.

Our brain waves vary continuously throughout the day, from moment to moment, and are dependent on

---

[4] Hans Berger (1873–1941) was a German psychiatrist who discovered the alpha wave rhythm. He noticed how the alpha rhythm was replaced by beta wave pattern when the subject's eyes opened.

what we are feeling, thinking or doing at a particular point in time. Nowadays these continuous EEG waveforms are easily measurable on small recording devices via scalp electrodes connected to computer laptops.

The electrical waveforms of the brain are dynamic. They vary continuously in accordance to their predominant component frequency at different levels of consciousness. In the alert state of consciousness, especially when we are attentive, focused and engaged in problem solving, beta waves predominate. When we close our eyes and enter into a meditative state, the mind calms down and alpha waves begin to appear more frequently. It is for this reason that the meditative state used to be known as the *alpha state*.

Alpha waves are of particular interest to us. In mindfulness, when the alpha frequency dominates, our sensory inputs tend to be at a minimum and our mind is generally free from unwanted thoughts. It is well known that mindfulness training has a tendency to help the individual produce more alpha waves. Increasingly nowadays, brain researchers are looking into how the alpha state attained through mindfulness can be used to build up the *power to ignore* as a means to battle symptoms of anxiety.

Alpha waves have also been scientifically studied for their association with creativity. These waves are particularly strong when the brain's visual cortex is resting with the eyes closed and the individual meditating. When we open our eyes, the alpha activity attenuates. Scientific research has shown that higher alpha brain activity correlates with the ability of people to come up with more innovative ideas.

For people experiencing deep relaxation, or undergoing hypnosis, the appearance of theta waves becomes obvious. The theta or deep hypnotic state is often used for therapy of mental and emotional issues. Lastly, for all of us in the dreamless sleep state, the brain waveforms will tend to slow down dramatically. In this state, the delta waves predominate.

Research of EEG waveforms in deep meditation has consistently shown an increase in the amplitude of lower EEG frequencies between 4 and 10 Hz. This corresponds to the theta band plus the lower end of the alpha band.

Transitoriness

People come and go in life,
They stay for a little while,
And go after a while.
They leave things behind,
A memory,
A change,
A difference,
A spark of love,
A past,
A lesson,
A lesson necessary in our lifetime,
To mould,
To shape,
To change,
To affect who we are.

By: Chong Jia Yi

Chapter Two

Instilling Inner Peace

Owing to our fast pace of living, most of us develop a tendency to waste our lives by distracting from our true selves with the endless activities that we engage in. In modern living, most of us fill our lives with an intense and anxious struggle for success. To do so, we arm ourselves with speed, intensity and aggression. This is often done in the spirit of a constantly competitive mode. We set our goals to achieve and strive to attain the outcomes we aim for. For school students, they constantly work towards high scores and good grades with the aim to outperform each other. To get into university, they juggle their available time between academic work, sports and extracurricular activities. This has become a very common and unconscious source of stress.

Competitive stress is very real in the school environment. In the area of sports, for instance, the student feels that his self-esteem is threatened during a competition. The stress comes about from an imbalance between the performance demands of the competition and the student's perception of his own ability to meet those demands successfully. Such stresses, although considered by many as necessary for growth and maturity, has a downside. They encourage us to develop an imbalance between our body and the mind, leading us into mental anxiety. The mind needs an inner environment of peace to be able to manage this stress. To this end, meditation is the recommended tool.

Mindfulness has been presented as a form of meditation in the previous chapter. However, it should be noted that the two are not exactly synonymous. Mindfulness is the power of our mind to give non-judgmental attention to our experience as it unfolds in a quiet environment. Meditation, on the other hand, refers to the exercises that we can use to enlarge and refine mindfulness. It is a way of retraining the mind. It provides us with specific ways to make our awareness into a discipline while putting us in a particular mental context to work at.

To retrain the mind, we must know the nature of how the mind works. To this end, the iceberg model helps to simplify our understanding.

Our mind can be conceived as having two parts: (a) a conscious mind which stays above the water level and is represented by the *tip of the iceberg*, and (b) an unconscious mind which is represented by the huge submerged component of the iceberg that lies below the water surface. The conscious mind deals with logic, reasoning, analysis and rationale while the unconscious mind handles the more abstract functions of thoughts, memories, emotions, feelings, intuition, creativity, innovativeness and dreams.

> *"That deep silence has a melody of its own, a sweetness unknown, admits the harsh discords of the world's sounds."*
>
> *– Paul Brunton*

To meditate is to be in harmony with our own existence. In a meditative or alpha state, we achieve a complete break from the normal stress of life. This state guides us to a freedom from unwanted concerns. In that mental state we are no longer concerned with the competitiveness in schoolwork, top grades in educational assessments or trophies from sport achievements.

Through mindfulness and the inner peace acquired, we are able to set aside our intense and anxious struggles.

Technique of Mindfulness Meditation

Mindfulness meditation practice starts with finding a quiet space and the time on a daily basis. The good news is that not a lot of time is needed. A beginner can start with just 10 minutes a day and gradually increase it to 20 to 30 minutes. When the benefits become obvious, the individual can begin to attach more importance to the practice and accord it priority. Many of us have no difficulty doing a sitting meditation for 45 minutes comfortably once we get into a regular routine.

Mindfulness is but one of many approaches to meditation. Strictly speaking, meditation is not something that someone can or cannot do. It is something that happens naturally. Meditation is simply speaking pure awareness to ourselves. It is the individual's presence in the here and now, unclouded by the dust of thoughts, emotions and desires, be they from the past or future. The mindfulness technique acts only as a key that opens the door to our consciousness to prepare us for meditation. It is not meditation itself.

In our growing years, our minds have been conditioned to being easily distracted. We therefore need to set aside a special place and time to minimise those distractions and to allow the mind to concentrate on learning *how* to concentrate. To create an environment for cultivating a calm and alert mind, the body posture must firstly be brought into a still and stable position.

To achieve peace of mind, our body must also be at peace. So, it is important to choose a position that will be comfortable for a long period of time. For this reason, sitting upright is recommended. The sitting lotus, or cross-legged position, is the traditional and recommended position. However, this may not necessarily be comfortable for people who have a past back injury. For that matter, we can feel free to choose to sit in any pose that we may be comfortable with. I personally take the view that the importance of getting into a meditative state quickly outweighs the need to learn to adapt to the traditional position slowly.

The physical effort to remain upright without additional support energises the meditation process. For people with back trouble, the use of a chair is acceptable. In addition, a cushion may be used to help to keep the spine straight. It is recommended that we wear loose, comfortable clothing and remember to remove our shoes while in that position. We do not want our blood circulation to get restricted during the process.

Traditionally, our arms and hands will find their place in two places. Either we rest our hands on our lap, with the palms facing upwards, one on top of the other, or we may wish to rest our hands on our knees, with the palms either facing up or down.

Meditation is not always about sitting down. The topic of walking meditation is addressed in a later chapter.

Primary Meditation Object

Mindfulness means constant awareness of an object, whatever that may be. We can divide them into primary and secondary objects for ease of discussion. Any object can be a meditation focus and our initial task is to be aware of it continuously. Subsequently we need to stay aware of one object arising after another.

We begin by keeping our eyes closed and our mind focused on a mental anchor of our choice, to help our mind settle down. Practically anything can be used, be it a candle's flame, someone's voice, a thought or even the feeling of our body sitting on the chair. A good and convenient anchor is to use our breathing as the primary meditative object, especially since it is always present with us. It is something we can always return to, whenever our mind wanders. Both the chest movement and the air motion change from moment to moment, and this provides an excellent dynamic object for us to anchor our attention and observations.

First, we focus our attention on the air entering our nostrils. Note its characteristics, including the sensation of the airflow and temperature. As we feel it moving down the throat and air passages, observe the expansion of the abdomen and chest all the way up to the level of our collar bones. Likewise, with the outgoing breath, notice and observe the pressure of the air leaving the chest and the associated contraction of the abdomen. As we breathe in, we say mentally in our mind, "*breathing in*". As we breathe out, we mentally say, "*breathing out*". We watch our breath as the exhalation comes to an end. We should remember not to change our usual pattern of breathing and to stay natural with it. Our job is only to observe what happens from moment to moment while being focused on an object. If we can do this, we are being mindful.

When we follow the above instructions, we have made breathing our *primary object*. However, this primary object is not the only meditation object. When other objects come into our attention, such as noises, body sensations, thoughts or feelings, we are going to take note of them. These are *secondary objects*. We do not shut ourselves off from them. It will not be possible for us to do that anyway.

Secondary Objects

As a beginner, you will find it very difficult to stay concentrated for long, no matter how hard you try. You will, after a short duration, experience a torrent of thoughts coming in and your mind begins to wander. When this happens, there is no necessity to feel anxious. Simply take note of the fact that your mind has strayed from its anchor, and gently bring your attention back to your breath. You may find yourself having to do this repeatedly in the beginning. However, do not be self-critical. It is a natural way of "taming" your mind. Don't give up and abandon the process when your mind wanders. Blaming yourself for the perceived failure would thwart the very serenity you are trying to build.

During a sitting meditation, it is not uncommon to find another object impinging strongly on our awareness. This tends to draw our attention away from our breathing movements. We must clearly note this secondary object. For instance, if we encounter a loud sound during our meditation, we may consciously direct our attention towards that sound as soon as it arises. We become aware of the sound as a direct experience, and when the sound fades off, we come back to focusing on the expansion of the abdomen and chest as part of our breathing movements, and as our primary object. This is the basic principle to follow.

From the meditation point of view, we live in six worlds: (1) the *seeing* world, (2) the *hearing* world, (3) the *touching* world, (4) the *smelling* world, (5) the *tasting* world and (6) the *thinking* world. If we hear a background conversation some distance away, we just focus on the direction of the voice and mentally say to ourselves: *"hearing, hearing, hearing"* a few times and bring our attention back to our breathing, which is our primary anchor. If we feel a painful sensation in a particular part of the body such as the knee, we may turn our attention to the joint for a moment and note it in our mind as "*pain, pain, pain*" for a few times, then leave it there and return to our breathing. It is not unusual to feel numb in the buttocks after sitting for a while. In such a situation, we should try to stay with it for as long as we can without changing posture. We make a mental note of "*numbness, numbness, numbness*", leave it there and come back to our breathing as the focus. Likewise, if the thought of difficult mathematical formulas that we learned in class surfaces, we simply note "*thinking, thinking, thinking*" and then return to our breath.

Many beneficial effects can be experienced with this simple exercise. Cultivating mindfulness in this way allows us to release all that we are grasping on to, be it our thoughts, feelings or body sensations. We let our body and mind drift into a state of stillness while relaxing our self into our true nature. With this moment-to-moment awareness, our mind opens up to another way of looking at our studies, our mental processes, our relationships and at our life as a whole.

Intriguingly, mindfulness helps to construct for us a perspective of not trying to freeze time. We will soon realise that each breath is a fleeting event. By watching how our breaths come and go, mindfulness reminds us not to hold on to our experiences as time flows by. The essence of the technique is one of *participatory observation*. In other words, the individual is both a participant and observer in the process. The essence of the perspective is that all phenomena are transitory and not permanent. This insight paves the way to inner peace.

Once attained, we allow our inner peace to work on us and to gather our scattered mind together. In the quiet of the meditative process, we will find ourselves awakened to our self-awareness with clarity. We may find ourselves watching our own emotions and body sensations and reviving past memories. At the same time, we also learn to feel the emotions underlying those memories.

The awareness attained in the mindful state is not intellectual in nature. We do not get involved with concepts or explanations surrounding those emotions or sensations. We do not get hung up on our past memories. Nor do we formulate any opinions about them. We just observe those memories as if they were occurring for the first time. We make no attempt to compare experiences, evaluate or categorise them. We do not ruminate on any of those past events. The awareness of those past experiences takes place in the here and now. It is the observation of what is happening in the present moment without judgment that enables us to set ourselves apart from our past experiences.

Staying Neutral

As meditators, we take a non-interference approach. We simply observe what is taking place. We do not refer to the observed experiences as belonging to us. If anything, we create an emotional distance between ourselves and the experience under observation.

As our meditation proceeds, we may discover that certain parts of our body need to be adjusted in position for increased comfort. If this need arises, it is perfectly alright to do so. The idea is not to remain absolutely still but to attain a reasonable amount of body stability to allow us to continue to focus on developing our moment-to-moment awareness.

We do not live in the same meditative world all the time. From the *seeing world*, our meditative mind may migrate to the *thinking world*, with a focus on our school studies, which has now become the meditative object. Like everyone else, we tend to make many things out of what we see, hear or think. When we make something out of it, what follows is our judgment. In the thinking world, we create unpleasantness or sadness through what we feel about our class performance. We experience disappointment and unhappiness about what we achieved in our exam, which has now become a secondary object. What we should do instead is to pay bare attention to our school results without judging.

Soon, with practice, we will find our negativity towards our studies and our life disarming, and our aggression dissolving. We may also find our confusion disappearing. However, let us not be mistaken. Mindfulness does not blot away things that have happened to us before. Nor are we training ourselves to ignore or forget them. Mindfulness helps us to get into a level of experience that is beyond feeling good or feeling bad. It is an opportunity for us to train ourselves to feel neither pleasurable about our past achievements nor painful about our past failures. It is a journey from *negativity to neutrality.*

With practice, we will find that the mindfulness technique helps to remind us to apply our attention to the proper object at the proper time and to exercise the correct amount of energy needed. When the correct amount of energy is applied, we will stay constantly in a state of calm and alertness.

In itself, meditation is less of a technique, but more of a process, a discipline and a journey. To meditate means to be a witness. It is a process of viewing, observing, reflecting and understanding ourselves. We need tools to help us to do so because that final understanding is deeply hidden within us. Meditation is the necessary tool to help us look inwards and reach to the point of our very life source. Once we touch that source, life becomes a celebration. This journey is possible because meditation is relaxed and has a passive, mirror-like quality of consciousness. In the beginning, we become more aware of the workings of all the layers of our mind, including our memories, our desires and our thoughts. When the awareness becomes so deep and so profound that it consumes the whole mind, we have reached the state where there is nothing to be aware of inside us.

Two Approaches

The above description has highlighted that two strategies or approaches to mindfulness meditation are currently being used. The first approach is that of *focused concentration*, that is, with our attention converged on the breath as the meditation object. The second approach is that of detached observation of our thinking and feeling processes. This is sometimes called *insight meditation*. Both approaches are relevant and important in the context of education and a school setting.

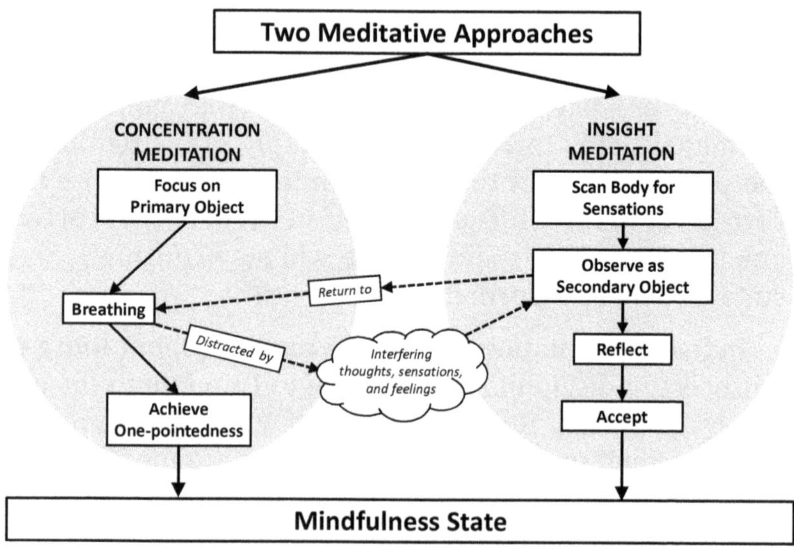

For a start we may want to practise these two processes separately, but with practice we can combine them in various ways. Both strategies have a common objective, and that is to retrain our power of attention. Doing so makes the mind peaceful. However, we are becoming increasingly aware that making the mind peaceful is not a sure thing because of interfering thoughts, sensations and feelings. Hence, we need the second approach to help us stay peaceful, despite distracting thoughts.

(a) Concentration Meditation

Concentration meditation is a state in which the mind is brought to rest, focused on one item and not allowed to wander. The technique is used to develop the stability and intensity of attention. Usually this type of meditation commences by focusing on the breath as the *primary* object. This method of concentration can take different forms. The focus can be on the in-breath and out-breath at the position of the nostril and nasal passage. Alternatively, the focus can be on the expansion and contraction of the chest, or the rising and falling of the abdomen.

Sometimes a *secondary* object is used when the chosen primary object becomes insignificant or difficult to perceive. Examples of secondary objects are body sensations. In the sitting posture, it is common to experience internal sensations such as tension in the spine and limbs that maintain the upright posture. More commonly, a skin itch may become a significant secondary object. There are also pressure sensations at the body surface such as where the dorsum of one hand is placed on top of the palm of the other or where the buttocks rest on the floor cushion or on the chair.

Sometimes the pressure sensation advances into a feeling of pain and the resulting pain sensation becomes the *primary* object when it becomes strong and persistent. As a rule, we should observe the pain sensation so long as we can maintain mindfulness satisfactorily despite the pain. When the severity of the pain is so high that we are unable to achieve mindfulness, then it is better for us to adjust or change our posture to continue being mindful.

Two mental faculties are needed in concentration meditation: mindfulness and introspection. In *mindfulness* there is no goal, no journey. We are just being mindful of what is happening there. There is no promise of any kind. *Introspection,* on the other hand, is a process of looking inwards to examine our own thoughts, feelings and emotion. It involves some kind of special reflection of our mental lives and, in the process, generates knowledge, judgment and beliefs about our own minds and current mental events. We can consider it as a form of quality control for which the process is necessary to police the mindfulness process.

At the start of the meditation, the attention is purposely maintained on the object chosen. Although we can intentionally concentrate on an image or the breathing process, there is a tendency to lose attention almost immediately or seconds later; especially for beginners. However, the ability to sustain the attention can be increased by cultivated insistence. This cultivated insistence is not a matter of increasing the power of concentration, but more of a motivation to stay persistently with the chosen image or object.

Peripheral noise or mental chatter will always interfere with our concentration process. With practice and the help of introspection, we achieve mental quietness until we reach the singular attention where our minds can focus on the selected object with stability and clarity for long periods. The mind behaves like a restless cow. Mindfulness helps the individual to acknowledge the restlessness, whereas introspection provides a big meadow space for the restless cow. In this manner mindfulness and introspection complement each other.

(b) Insight Meditation

Insight meditation takes us a step further. It helps us to cultivate a clear awareness of what is happening as it happens. Unlike *concentration meditation* in which the mind is pinned onto an object, *insight meditation* trains us to use mindfulness to help us to get a good look at the object carefully and thoroughly, and take note of how its features change with time.

The insight approach is really about mindful observation. The concept is similar to a scientist making close, detailed observations of his research subject continuously. During meditation we observe various aspects of our body with concentrated awareness. It is not just observing the rising and falling of our abdomen and chest as we breathe, but also the pressure of the chair on our buttocks, the aching sensation of thigh and calf muscles with prolonged sitting, the occasional itch over various skin surfaces and the various thoughts that flash into the mind during the meditative process.

This part of mindfulness practice trains us to be prepared to face the unexpected things in our day-to-day life. Under normal circumstances when we do not expect certain things to occur, it is very difficult to accept them as outcomes. As a result, we keep resisting. When we are mindful, not only can we observe what we visualise or feel, but we are also prepared to accept what we have not thought of before. For instance, we may not have anticipated our failure to come up with a piece of creative artwork in our school assignment. We cannot force ourselves not to react to our disappointment of failure, but we can train ourselves to simply observe our reaction – how we get discouraged or get disheartened. When we focus on observation instead of reaction, we come to see both the over-expected and the unexpected, and learn to live with the latter.

The aim of this insight approach is to look deeply within ourselves. When we start to observe, we will realise that our mind is a wild, thought-generating machine. Sometimes the thoughts are related to our problems at hand; sometimes they come out of nowhere. Soon we will realise all these thoughts and sensations that we are watching are constantly changing. They are not permanent. They come and go and are not within our conscious control. With insight meditation we learn to abandon the inclination to cling on to a false sense of things as being permanent. We also start to gain insight into what and who we really are, as an individual being, and the things we have no control over.

Mindfulness also helps the student to develop an innovative mind. The expertise that he already carries within him seldom leaves room for new possibilities or novelty within familiar situations. With the existing domain knowledge he possesses, he needs to be disciplined in his awareness of how he shuts off new ideas and possibilities. Many of us tend to believe that these ideas have been tried before and our experience suggests that it would not work.

> *"Do not seek the truth; only cease to cherish opinions."*
>
> *– A Zen poem by Seng-ts'an.*

With mindfulness, we learn to resist being dismissive or sceptical about our thoughts and ideas. We become aware of what we are thinking and how we are reacting to new ideas that we hear from others. We learn not to judge ideas based on our own experience and expectations. We avoid consciously dismissing the assumptions popping up in our thought-generating machine, and open our mind to the possibility that, yes, this idea could work. With practice we learn to think differently about ideas and concepts we have seen before. This is how we cultivate our innovative mindset.

Battling the Wandering Mind

The wandering mind is notorious as being a perpetual source of interference in meditation. We often find that after attempting to focus on our breathing for a few minutes, our mind does not want to stick on to the meditation object. We would rather think about something else such as "What will happen in class tomorrow?", "What is the teacher going to teach in the next Geography lesson?", "How well will I perform in my coming gymnastic competition?" or "What will Mom cook for dinner this evening after school?"

Such interfering thoughts are extremely common and are examples of human desire. In immersing ourselves in these desires, we generally miss the point that we simply do not know what will happen in the future. Desire is always aimed at something that is understood as good for the individual. The thoughts come from within. We always want what we believe to be good. We may find that, after a while, we do not wish to concentrate on our breath anymore because our breath is too simple. We find it too monotonous. We prefer to think about other things that are more intriguing and more interesting. Once we can accept the fact that we do get distracted now and again, it becomes easier to bring ourselves back to our meditation object, the breath. This is how we take care of our mind using the insight approach.

There is a second category of mental distraction. These are unfavourable thoughts arising out of unwholesome states which cloud the mind. Anger is one example. Our wandering thoughts may involve a past memory that is painful and that evokes our anger, perhaps with someone who has bullied us. Sometimes we may find our mind sluggish or sleepy. Occasionally, the mind is restless and provides fertile ground for more wandering thoughts. At other times we may be in doubt, delusion or conceit: "What is the point of struggling hard to get into university? I am tired and bored. I can easily succeed in my career without a degree." Such mental states make our mind impure.

In itself, a thought is harmless unless we believe in it. Many people think that thoughts of unpleasant situations or events make us suffer. In fact, it is the attachment to the thoughts that makes us suffer. When we are attached to a thought it simply means that we believe it is true without inquiring. We tend to think that we are what our thoughts tell us we are. When we practise mindfulness, we are on an exploratory trip to being open to possibilities beyond what we assume or think we know. It is about discovering our *don't-know mind*. We ask a question and let the answer finds us.

In real life, the truth is whatever is really happening in front of us. As an example, the thought that "my teacher should be more caring" may arise in the student's mind. This comes about because he believes it is true. With mindfulness, we allow the truth to rise within us by asking, "Can I know for certain that this is true?" Often, we tell ourselves that the statement appears to be true. Of course, it does. This is because our concept is based on a lifetime of uninvestigated beliefs. We react with an uncomfortable feeling, and with mental imagery to convince ourselves that the thought is true. We enter into a world that doesn't exist and stay in a stressed physical body that sees things through fearful eyes.

One of the powerful techniques we can learn from mindfulness meditation is to unravel for ourselves the cause and effect of a thought. We picture ourselves to be standing in front of the person who does not possess the thought. We ask: "How would our life be different in the same situation without the thought?" We keep our eyes closed and visualise what we will be like without this

Story of Self.[5] We will then come up with the answer, "I will be more peaceful" or "I will be clear enough to understand the situation and move on". Without the *Story of Self,* we are able to act clearly and fearlessly. Through mindfulness, we remind ourselves that we are a friend and a listener to our self.

Quite often, with a torrential flow of wandering thoughts in the initial stages, we may not always get into a meditative state. In such a situation it is usually because three things are lacking. Firstly, our *mindfulness level* is too low. For that we need to remember to keep reminding ourselves that our breath is the primary meditation object. Secondly, we need *faith* in ourselves. We need to believe that we have enough concentration power to do it. Thirdly, we need *effort* to support our mindfulness. We require to continually push ourselves to focus our awareness on our in-breath and out-breath. We must reassure ourselves that if we persist, we will be successful in attaining concentration within a short time.

Many people use wandering thoughts as a reason for giving up meditation after their first few attempts. They fail to realise that these thoughts do not automatically appear during meditation. They come because we want the wandering thoughts for ourselves. The thoughts are caused by our desires. We find the repetitive breathing motion monotonous and we have a desire to go somewhere else that is more interesting. Hence, our mind gets stuck onto more attractive objects which we may find elsewhere. Once stuck, our wandering mental images will appear and draw us away from our breath. Likewise, once we set our intention that we do not want to contact

---

[5] The *Story of Self* is essentially a story that we share with others to enable them to experience the source of values that motivates us to act in a certain manner. The story presents a specific challenge that we face and the choice we made about how to deal with the challenge. Often, by sharing the story it connects others with us.

these objects while we meditate, the wandering thoughts and images will not arise.

The main reason for a wandering mind is because all of us like to be free and relaxed with a pleasurable surrounding. Our mindfulness level is not strong enough to adhere to the meditation object, which is our breath. We always expect to be surrounded with sensual desires and have contact with pleasant feelings. We want to feel comfortable in our own enjoyable way and we do not want to set boundaries for our wandering mind. We adopt the never-mind attitude and tell ourselves: "Let it be". This explains why we feel happy when we are in touch with greed, and why we follow this desire regardless of whether we get what we want or not.

> *"Meditation is not a way of making your mind quiet. It's a way of entering into the quiet that's already there – buried under the 50,000 thoughts the average person thinks every day."*
>
> *— Deepak Chopra*

In the beginning, we may have to struggle and struggle. Our mind may go out again and again with wandering thoughts and we have to pull it back again and again, perhaps feeling a bit tiring. Then we may fall asleep in the process. Again, we need to wake up each time fighting with our impure mind. However, we do not run away from the problem; we just face and accept it. After we become used to it, we will find that our mind becomes alert, calm and happy. Such acceptance is possible through the development of constant awareness.

Once the feeling of happiness comes about, concentration improves. With concentration, clarity improves. In time, the mind enters into an absorbed state and is able to stop concentrating on the breathing. We find that we can let go of the breath, relax and yet retain our awareness of our meditative state. This is when we reach one-pointedness of the mind. In this state, our mind is not distracted by wandering thoughts anymore.

Desire for a Goal

The initial training of the mind starts with a goal. The goal is what empowers us to succeed in mindfulness meditation. If we do not have a goal, we will not set up the desire to achieve that goal and there will be no results. Our mind will wander around and we do not reach that one-pointedness state.

The trick of reaching the one-pointedness state is to learn to be peaceful, relaxed and happy with our breath. As students in biological science we learn that the breathing movement is both a controllable act of the conscious mind and an autonomic process that continues without conscious awareness. From a psychology perspective, our breathing functions as an interface between our conscious and our unconscious mind. By operating on this interface, we can easily gain access into the depths of the unconscious mind to find peaceful relaxation, happiness and compassion.

There are many benefits of meditation besides enhancing our brain capacity and learning abilities. The practice reduces our emotional distress with our schoolwork and improves our mood and behaviour. It helps us to focus and concentrate on our studies. We can quit our bad habits easier. We accept ourselves better and find our relationships harmonise better. With constant practice we will experience the sense of oneness in ourselves while our wisdom and awareness grow.

Mindfulness also helps us to handle our past better. We become better at letting go of our unpleasant past. However, being mindful doesn't mean that we should forget what has once existed. Bad things or failures may have happened in the past, and if we use the past to judge ourselves and others we run into problems of anxiety.

History is a prominent feature of a person's life. We need to be aware of our historical past to make better judgments in the present. But what we shouldn't do is to make ourselves scared of studying for fear of making similar mistakes. The past has a powerful way of convincing us that we have created a precedent that is unchangeable and will repeat itself. We tend to fall victim to that notion. What mindfulness teaches us is that we cannot control the past, and the only moment we have is *now*. While we know we have taken a different path in the past, we also know that we have power, *in this moment*, to select a route to make a positive change in our life.

How will the Mindfulness process Unfold?

As we begin from where we are and maintain a regular practice, we will realise that we do not have to live life in a self-alienated manner any longer. We can achieve not only calmness but also bliss. Bliss is a state of perfect happiness and being oblivious of everything else.

As our efforts continue, we will realise that there is another way to view life and reality apart from the way we have always done. We will come to understand that our problems of stress and unhappiness are based on a fear that is unfounded. We will find that we are becoming less sensitive and less anxious.

As insights crop up during our quiet and peaceful moments, we are no longer so rushed in our study pace nor so defensive against criticisms from our teachers. Feeling reassured as we grow with the practice, we find ourselves staying more and more in the present moment, with less anxiety about the uncertain future. We will soon realise that we do not have to trust or depend on others to support our confidence. We feel safe, joyful and surrounded by love as we build up our sense of clarity and fulfilment.

Guided Mindfulness Meditation

Guided meditation is the practice of using spoken words, mental imagery and serene music to help an individual access the subconscious mind. Nowadays, it is increasingly popular for people to listen to guided meditation scripts, especially when they are now widely available on YouTube. With the help of headphones, many beginners find themselves more likely to remain focused when they follow the instructive voice.

In fact, with a guided meditation, we do not even need to know how to meditate. All that is required is to listen and flow with the instruction, and we will move effortlessly into the serenity of the unconscious mind. An example of a guided mindfulness script is given in Appendix I.

Mindfulness Retreat

With regular practice many of us would probably find it comfortable to integrate meditation along with our studies, work and all the other things we do in our daily life. However, some of us find that we need a break from our routine to maximise the benefit. When we are on a retreat, we have time and space away from our daily distractions because all we do is meditating.

A retreat is a "drawback" to consciously set aside time for a change in focus in our life. It is a deliberate act of stepping outside our routine by withdrawing from the stresses and pressures of our daily schedule to be in a quiet place where our senses are open to rediscover ourselves. The purpose is to give us a new environment to see things and open up new possibilities. Silence is usually a significant component of a retreat, and this is more than just not speaking. It involves the recognition of a quiet depth in each of us that allows things to arise and flow through the mental landscape It is a great way to renew ourselves, physically and mentally.

A mindfulness retreat is a particularly great way for newcomers and beginners to learn the meditation technique quickly. Seasoned practitioners, on the other hand, can also learn to go deeper and strengthen their practice during retreats. We commonly find that meditation retreats make us feel that our aloneness is not quite so lonely. We learn to drop limiting beliefs, regrets and worries. We also learn to tap into a bigger vision of ourselves.

Once an active, outgoing English language teacher in her early thirties went for a two-day meditation retreat in Thailand and it turned out to be a life-changing event for her. She shared her unexpected experience with me:

> *"The two-day-one-night silent meditation retreat must have been the toughest challenge for me as an avid traveller. I learned sitting, walking, lying down and hand movement meditations all during the short retreat. What I particularly enjoyed was the self-development and better control of my mind; in other words, staying focused in the present and not dwelling over the past or future events. I am elated to experience inner happiness and am ready to conquer new challenges in my life. It doesn't stop here; I'll continue the journey to master inner peace. The best lesson I've learned during the retreat is: Let it happen, let it go."*

A sense of how our progress in mindfulness meditation may unfold over a longer period may be appreciated from the diary of a medical-school teacher who went for a ten-day retreat in Malaysia. In a quiet secluded area, he stayed in a simple dormitory, surrendered his mobile phone and reading materials and took a vow of silence. He then sat down to meditate for eleven hours a day. He recalled his experiences after the retreat as follows:

> ***Day 1*** *– My mind was wandering wildly. The thoughts were very random and were mostly about recent events at work and home. Getting up at 4:00 am was all right but remaining awake with focused meditation from 4:30 to 6:30 am was tough.*
>
> ***Day 2*** *– I was able to focus better and for longer duration before the mind started to wander. However, I was able to gain awareness of my wandering mind sooner than the previous day. I started to relish the time that I was not meditating to reflect on various issues. I had trouble sleeping in the night. My dreams were very vivid, and somewhat macabre. I wonder if it is because my subconscious mind had become more stimulated?*
>
> ***Day 3*** *– I was able to hold my concentration for a much longer period. Body sensations came readily and I noted ripples of skin sensation moving across my upper lip. I also noticed myself falling into a surreal zone when I was in full concentration. It was almost like being in a suspended state of consciousness where only those sensations were felt. It was on one of these occasions that I saw flashes of bright light.*
>
> ***Day 4*** *– My right leg was really hurting after prolonged sitting during the last three days. I must have compressed a nerve as the outer aspect of the leg and foot were numbed. It was difficult to find a less painful position to sit and I kept shifting many times during a one-hour meditation.*
>
> ***Day 5*** *– In between the shifting of the sitting position, I was increasingly aware of the sensations of my body.*

These mostly felt like involuntary contraction of the muscles as they were like twitching. When I focused on the left leg, I felt waves of electric currents going down. I started to think about the technique of Vipassana (Insight Meditation). I began to understand it as the developing of awareness of the firing of the nerves as represented by the tingling sensations.

Days 6 & 7 – *The main challenge during these two days was to find a comfortable position which allowed me to meditate for longer durations before being distracted by the pain. Upon realising that I was unable to be objective about the pain, I just "watched" the pain. It was too excruciating. At last, I found a position that I could sit without shifting for an hour towards the end of day 7. This was also when I could sweep my awareness of body sensation from head to toe for the first time.*

Day 8 – *On this day I noticed more and more fine sensations were being felt. By lunch time, I was noticing the tingles all over the body except for the chest. After lunch I tried hard to focus on detecting the fine tingles over the chest area but got increasingly frustrated by my failure. I was craving for the sensations and was disappointed by the lack of results. Then I reflected on the purpose of the meditation exercise, which included developing equanimity and awareness of impermanence of the experience. After this I was able to calm the mind. Just before tea-break at 5:00 pm I started to feel the tingles all over the chest and abdomen. I freely scanned my body sensations from head to toe. It was an epiphany. The wisdom of this meditation technique was so real and experiential. Then I broke down and sobbed, upon the realisation of how this can be so applicable to life. Fortunately, by then, most* *of the other participants had left the meditation hall and proceeded to the dining room for the tea-break and I don't think they saw me crying.*

Day 9 – *While I was able to scan the body from head to toe to observe the fine body sensations the day before, I seemed to have lost the ability on Day 9. I have also lost awareness of the gross sensations. It seemed like my mind was not as focused anymore. Perhaps I was getting complacent or proud. Learning from the lesson of the experience the day before, I remained equanimous about my observation. I told myself that I have done it before, that I know how it felt like and that I will eventually be able to do it again. I went back to practise the steps that I have learned from Day 1 onwards and slowly progressed. By evening, I was once again able to sweep freely from head to toe, and toe to head in observing my sensations.*

Day 10 – *I was glad that the retreat was almost over. I was actually quite comfortable over the last ten days not talking to anyone after taking a vow of silence. I ate less than what I normally do and led a simple life. The toughest part was waking up early in the morning to meditate. I was also relishing the time I had to myself and be in tune to my own body sensations. I felt and sounded funny when I broke the vow and spoke for the first time in ten days. After that, the conversations flowed freely, and everyone in the group retreat was just eager to know more about each other.*

We are living in the age of the mobile smartphone, which means we are constantly bombarded by emails, announcements, newsfeed and WhatsApp messages from colleagues and friends. We are also inclined to act on them instantly. The impact of this constant chatter means that the mind is never calm enough to identify the negative influences in our lives, let alone finding solutions to get rid of them. By surrendering his mobile phone and staying disconnected and silent, the participant was able to emerge from the retreat with more clarity and focus.

Everyday Mindfulness

Mindfulness is not just another name for sitting-down meditation. There is a second aspect to it, and that is about engaging our everyday task in a mindful way. *Everyday mindfulness* involves being fully aware, present and alert to the tasks and activities we carry out day-to-day, including eating, walking, learning, listening or establishing a conversation. In these situations, we are mindfully attuned to our inner thoughts and feelings as well as our external sensory experience.

In mindful eating, we pay full attention to the piece of food we have selected to eat, how it looks, how it smells and how we have selected to cut it. We are also mindful of the arm muscles we use to raise it to our mouth, and the texture and taste of the food as we chew it. Likewise, in mindful walking, we take note of the feel of the ground under our feet and the changing pressure on our soles as we move forward with each step. We would observe our breathing as we walk and feel the freshness of the air around us. We sense the temperature on our skin, look at the sky and observe other walkers around us in the park. The same principles are applicable to the concept of mindful learning.

Mindful Learning

Many of our beliefs about the learning process are mindsets that have been accepted to be true. Whenever we want to learn something new, be it a new subject matter, a musical instrument or a sporting skill, we paradoxically rely on ways of learning that typically work to our detriment, or a state of mindlessness.

One common mindset is *learning by repetition*. We repeat a process over and over again as a routine in a learning process until we rely on the repetition mindset to achieve our learning goal. When we learn by repetition, we come to rely on the mindset that the basics should be learned so well until they become our second nature. We rely on decisions made and distinctions drawn in the past. Once we do that, our mental state becomes stuck in a single perspective and oblivious to different contexts in which the meaning conveyed by a particular piece of information may change.

A second way of generating mindlessness in the educational environment takes place during the initial exposure of the person to the information. When the student is first given the information, he is taught to process it without questioning alternative ways of understanding it. In processing the information mindlessly, he takes the information in as true without asking under what conditions it may not be true. This is generally the way that most people learn things and is also why people are frequently in error but rarely in doubt.

Unfortunately, most of our modern teaching methods continue to foster mindless ways of learning. Teachers present facts as closed packages without attention to looking at them from different perspectives. A common example is that of scientific research findings. Although research evidences are usually presented in textbooks as probabilities, they are often translated into absolute statements that hide the uncertainties in the findings. In truth, the facts derived from scientific research are to be understood in their context and their meaning, and their usefulness is highly dependent on the situation. Because of the way facts are presented in the classroom, it seldom presents opportunities for the student to ask pertinent questions.

Visualisation and Guided Imagery

Guided imagery is sometimes regarded as the lazy guy's way of practicing meditation. It is a passive activity where the practitioner simply listens to a prescriptive set of verbal instructions. With the headphones on, the individual hits the play button and focuses on the voice, the evocative language of the script, the soothing music and the mental images created. With the assisted environment he finds himself carried to his own inner experience. The process requires much less discipline than the traditional sitting meditation.

With guided imagery, we tap into the power of our own imagination and construct an immersed state of mind by visualising all five senses changing. This approach is suitable for beginners. However, sometimes mental imagery also occurs in a deeply meditating and relaxed individual who can form mental imagery without consciously willing it. The imagery in such a situation may carry pertinent symbolic messages and can be used to increase learning and comprehension of our life issues.

A man in his mid-thirties was once in a depressed mood and asked for guidance and life directions. He had been facing a lot of stress in his fast-paced job in the finance sector while also being in the midst of a marriage crisis. After he learned the basics of mindfulness, he was soon able to get into a meditative state with self-guided mental imagery. On his own he started to visualise mental imagery which he found meaningful.

> *Yesterday, during the morning meditation, I experienced a set of vivid imagery for a split second, like a sudden flash. I see myself standing outside a window staring in. it is daytime and sunny outside.*

There is a light green curtain on the inner side of the window. The wind is blowing, and the curtain flapping. The right half of the curtain is pulled all the way to the edge, but the left curtain is stretched out, about a third of the way across the window. The wind is blowing and the curtain tussling beautifully and peacefully in the air. Inside the room I see a chair next to the wall, with the seat facing me. It is a very simple chair and is empty. It looks grey in colour and has a very basic metal frame. The light from outside illuminates the room and I can see clearly the interior, but it is not as bright as compared to when the fluorescent lights are turned on. There is nothing special about the room or the chair; it actually feels quite lonely and deserted. However, the flapping curtain is beautiful and calming.

I reflected on that lonely room with the chair and the lovely curtain blowing in the wind. I sensed that the chair is mine to sit on so that I can look out at the window. The empty room feels almost like a prison. Then I see myself sitting in the chair, looking out. Beyond the window I can see a dirty road emerging and fading out to the horizon. Then at the point where the horizon meets the perfect blue sky, some snow-capped mountains emerge.

I sense yearning, as well as some sadness. I sense that the room represents me somehow; empty and cold. Then the other me who can move around freely is also me. The me who can move wants to escape but it is not easy to. The view from the inside is one of despair.

A gentle breeze blows into the room. It is warm, comforting and just the right temperature. It feels as if there is a texture to the wind, and the curtain, beautiful and soothing, is there to comfort and accompany me. Its presence seems to be a reminder

> *of what I could not see but could feel through that gentle breeze. I don't think I want to be in that room or cell, but it feels familiar. The emotion it evoked feels familiar.*

The guided imagery described in the above example appears to be self-generated rather than prescribed. However, the technique can still be considered as a form of guided meditation. It helps the practitioner to learn how to relax and release himself from his moment-to-moment fixation on the content on his mind. By cultivating a detachment, it becomes easier for him to observe the stressful thoughts streaming from the mind. In that conducive environment, the practitioner utilises all his meditative senses – sight, hearing, touch, smell, taste and thinking – to build images in the mind, so much so that he can feel the imagery as if it is a real external event.

There is a slight difference between visualisation and guided imagery. In visualisation we focus purely on the visual sense. In guided imagery, however, we construct an immersed state of mind throughout the body by feeling changes in all the six senses. The multisensory characteristic of the process helps the practitioner to get in touch with the subconscious wisdom within him. Once there, he is able to envision himself being placed in an enlightened state where he is more prepared to face a life lesson.

The Lesson

Remember, it's always good,
Always good,
To let us continue our journey,
To become a better version of ourselves,
A version of us that we want to be,
We have a choice as to what we take and get,
From each lesson,
And each person in our lives.

As we live, as we love, as we grow,
As we break uncomfortably,
And painfully out of our shell each time,
Get acquainted with that pain,
That uncomfortable feeling,
As it is a sign that we're growing,
Loving to be back with ourselves,
A full circle.

By: Chong Jia Yi

Chapter Three

An Evolving Concept

Whenever the subject of mindfulness meditation is talked about, the image of the silhouette of a person sitting in the lotus position comes to mind or is introduced. Commonly this image calls to mind a representation of a yogi or a Buddhist monk. As such, the question often asked is whether mindfulness is a spiritual ritual, or if it has origins from a religion.

In truth, mindfulness meditation is the product of an ancient Indian tradition that goes back earlier than the time of Buddhism. The earliest evidence of the practice of meditation was found in the Indus Valley civilisation which peaked during 3000–2500 BC[6] and was later rediscovered, redeveloped and expanded on by Siddhartha Gautama. While meditation is not a Buddhist invention, Gautama Buddha had undoubtedly studied the technique in great detail and advanced its understanding. He certainly deserves to be given credit for having studied it in depth and taught it widely to his followers.

Etymology

To understand mindfulness in its present-day form, it is necessary to re-visit the underpinnings of the concept in its early tradition. Examining the origin of the word *mindfulness* gives us an insight to the profoundness of the

[6] *History of Mindfulness*, by Bhikkhu Sujato, 2012, p 153.

practice. The term *mindfulness* was originally coined by a Professor of Pali in the University of London, T.W. Rhys Davids.[7] He deliberated on various terms before settling for one that did not have any reference to "enlightenment" nor any connotation to religious esotericism.

In brief, the concept of mindfulness originated from the Pali word *sati* or Sanskrit word *smrti*, both of which have three components in their meaning: *awareness, concentration* and *memory*. However, the meaning of "memory" here does not refer to recalling the past, but paradoxically to remembering the present, and reminding ourselves of whatever we are experiencing from moment to moment. This meaning is also well captured in the character used in Chinese translation: ⍰. The character is made up of two parts and refers to the act of putting our heart and mind (⍰) on the present, (⍰).

The term *sati* is used in the ancient text in two senses: firstly, to remember or recollect, and secondly, to bear in mind. The element of *remembering* has stemmed from a mental culture of memorising long sacred texts during those early days. To do so efficiently, it was necessary to repeat passages over and over again. However, if memorising was done in a mechanical manner, there would be a lack of interest on the part of the individual and the memory process would likely fail. In an effort to increase the effectiveness of recall, the individual had to bring in attention, inspiration, joy and understanding of his memory task. To achieve this, the person learned to stay with the present moment. This is perhaps where we see the link between the meaning of *sati* with the idea of *mindfulness*. In terms of function, the word *sati* was used to map out a process of developing a healthy mind.

---

[7] T.W. Rhys Davids (1843–1922) was the son of a clergyman, a British scholar of the Pali language and founder of the Pali Text Society.

Following the Buddhist development of mindfulness, the teachings have since found their way to the West and to Western secular helping practices. In 1881, Rhys Davids decided to adopt "mindfulness" as the formal English translation of *sati*. This was slowly absorbed into the English lexicon and spread throughout the secular world over the following century. By 1910 the word mindfulness had become the accepted translation of sati.

Starting in the late 19th century, the concept of mindfulness was popularised by a Burmese insight movement that aimed to take meditation out of the monasteries and disseminate it to the general population. By the late 20th century this was well developed and established. Mahāsī Sayādaw,[8] U Ba Khin[9] and S.N. Goenka[10] were the main figures involved.

By the 1960s the practice of meditation based on Zen Buddhism had influenced the thinking of a number of leading psychotherapists in the West, the most notable of which is Dr Jon Kabat-Zinn,[11] a molecular biologist by training. He is credited as a key person in introducing mindfulness meditation to Western healthcare and psychotherapy. He developed the MBSR (Mindfulness-Based Stress Reduction) programme as an intervention that employs mindfulness practices for stress management. His approach has since been adapted as a

---

[8] Mahāsī Sayādaw (1904–82) was a Burmese Theravada Buddhist monk and meditation master.

[9] U Ba Khin (1899–1971) was the first Accountant General of the Union of Burma, known for his influential leadership on the Vipassana movement.

[10] S.N. Goenka (1924–2013) was a Burmese-born Indian businessman who suffered from migraine and resorted to Vipassana meditation for relief. He was trained under U Ba Khin and credited for bringing the meditation technique back to India in 1969.

[11] Jon Kabat-Zinn, (born 1944) studied meditation with Thich Nhât Hanh and founded the Stress Reduction Clinic at the University of Massachusetts Medical School in 1979.

cognitive behavioural intervention and is especially useful when researchers need to objectively analyse the active mechanisms and measure the benefits of mindfulness for the purpose of controlled clinical trials.

Classical Concept

When classical literature is examined, it is found that *sati* is used together with a verb which means *standing close* and *staying present*. The concept of *sati* is therefore understood as a quality that watches over the mind closely and reminds us of its presence. As an example, when we move from the train platform over a gap and step into the train carriage, there is often a warning label with the words: *Mind the Gap*. This mindful label makes us more aware of a potential risk of getting a foot stuck in the gap. Precisely, this act of bearing in mind the risk of entering and exiting a train during the moment of transit is what is being referred to as "remembering" in the concept and context of mindfulness.

Beyond the idea of remembering and observing what happens to us, the word *sati* also connotes the concepts of *awareness* and *attention*.

Awareness

Awareness can be thought of as the background radar of our consciousness and monitors our inner and outer environment. *Attention,* on the other hand, is the process of focusing our conscious awareness by providing heightened sensitivity to a limited range of experiences. The word *sati* has an earthly quality in that it refers to the grounding of the person to give him some stability of the mind. Once steady, *sati* functions as the gatekeeper for the mindfulness practitioner.

Recently, I visited the city of Jingzhou (⍰⍰) in China and observed the beauty of its famous ancient city wall. While observing the city gates, the traffic flow through those gates suddenly caught my attention because it struck me as an excellent analogy for understanding the concept of *sati*.

The city itself represents the physical body and mind. The various wall gates represent our biological senses of vision, hearing, smell, touch and taste while the gatekeeper and traffic controller represent *sati*. The city is exposed to the outside world through the gates while the gatekeeper of our biological senses mediates between the city and the outside world, checking the flow of traffic as it enters and leaves the city with discrimination.

This analogy illustrates the role of *sati* in "remembering" the present in mindful states. However, the reader must note that the *present* that sati remembers is the "experienced present" and not the "momentary present". In other words, the *present* is experienced as a continuously unfolding duration, and not just a single moment.

Attention in School

Attention is a process whereby we, as students, are able to select from among the many competing stimuli present in our school environment. This selective processing can be driven by our classroom goals, such as to follow an instruction from our teacher, to work out a problem using a mathematical formula, to dissect and understand a logical argument or to appreciate a humorous comment from a witty professor. Alternatively, we may be looking for a schoolmate we have lost in the crowd during recess period, in which case we pay attention to her long hair tied up in a bun and try to catch the sound of her voice in the crowd.

Often, in a school environment there is too much information at any given moment for students to cope with. We therefore select the most important information for further processing. However, at any one time, there is only a limited amount of information that we are capable of processing. Therefore, our goals and our salience of information direct us to what we pay attention to.

When new information arrives in a rapid stream, spending time processing it will cause us to miss some other incoming information. This failure to attend to information in space or time is a result of our learning system preventing us from being overloaded with irrelevant information. It is a system of selective attention. Concentration on one source of signal input to the exclusion of other sources is known as *focused attention.*

Usually when more than one source of information is attended to, the information selected or acquired is imperfect. This is because in divided attention, the two sources of information vie for limited attentional resources. We each have a pool of attentional effort into which each task taps. The more tasks there are at any one time, the more mental effort is drawn from the pool. When the available mental capacity is less than that required for completion of the task, failure occurs. This is why the idea of multi-tasking has been erroneously promoted these days.

Multi-tasking is about handling more than one task at the same time. It is a common sight to see people answering a WhatsApp message on their mobile phone while walking across the pedestrian crossing on the street or talking on the office phone while answering an email on the desktop computer at the same time. The benefits of multi-tasking have been overemphasised. It has been marketed as a great way to get many things done at once. People who multi-task at work are regarded as efficient and motivated employees. However, although it seems like many things are being accomplished simultaneously, our mind is not as good at handling multiple tasks as we like to believe.

Research has shown that multi-tasking can reduce productivity by as much as 40 per cent. What happens is that the person is quickly shifting his attention from task to task and his focus shifts from one thing to the next. Switching from one task to another makes it difficult to filter out distractions. It results in mental blocks that slow down performance. For a long time, it was believed that people who multi-tasked had an edge over those who did not. However, research has shown that multi-tasking actually decreases the effectiveness of learning. Students lose time as they switch between multiple learning tasks.

So, what makes a student a more effective learner? And, how can we help to improve his memory?

For a start, keep in mind that attention is a major component of memory. For the classroom information to move from the student's short-term memory to long-term memory, he needs to actively attend to the information input. Getting rid of distractions is paramount. What also helps is for him to visualise the information he is studying. Paying special attention to the charts and graphics in the textbooks is of tremendous help, and mindfulness has a role in developing this skill. He can even create his own visual cues and draw charts or figures in his mind as he reviews the information input.

Next, keep in mind that meditation helps to access the untapped subconscious memory stores. Research has shown that meditation stimulates memory, which is associated with a certain brain region, the hippocampus.[12] People who meditate regularly show a

---

[12] The hippocampus is a brain structure located in the temporal lobe below the cortex. The word comes from a Greek word meaning "sea-

higher level of theta activity in the hippocampus.[13] Meditation also stimulates the frontal lobe, which is associated with planning, problem-solving and emotional expression in addition to memory.

Evolution into Therapeutics

Patients with anxiety and needing help from the psychotherapist are often those who are preoccupied with past or future events. This is where the present-orientation of mindfulness is useful as a therapeutic tool.

People are depressed often because they feel regretful or sad over their past. A successful student may feel guilty because his other family members have been coping with major crises of unemployment and unpaid bills while he is enjoying academic work. He may be asking himself if it is morally correct for him to try to succeed when other family members are failing in life. Should the student decide to sacrifice himself for the family, further problems would arise. He may learn to resent his family members later because he feels deprived of an educational opportunity and becomes envious of his more successful schoolmates.

Whenever mindfulness is used as a tool in psychotherapy, patients are taught ways of developing a different relationship between themselves and the content of their experience. This is where *participatory observation* of their thoughts, emotions or cravings in the meditative state has much relevance and application.

---

horse", because of its shape. This part of the brain plays a crucial role in memory consolidation. It is commonly attacked in Alzheimer's disease.

[13] Anna Lardone et al. "Mindfulness Meditation Is Related to Long-Lasting Changes in Hippocampal Functional Topology during Resting State: A Magnetoencephalography Study." *Neural Plasticity*, Article ID 5340717
Vol 2018, https://doi.org/10.1155/2018/5340717

Many people are anxious because they fear the future and hate their past. By straying away from the present moment, their suffering increases. As they get absorbed with the mental activity and feelings of the past event, they begin to daydream and may get into a self-pity mode. They feel as if they are stuck watching the movie of their lives. In this situation, mindfulness can help them to step out of their conditioned mind and see things as they actually are.

Many students have sacrificed their schooling opportunity to enter the workforce early in the belief that it would help to ease their family's financial status. The truth is that, by suspending his academic journey, the self-sacrifice would last only as long as the family is in crisis. In the end, he will get to understand that by completing his college and university studies he will benefit his family in several ways. He will see that he will be in a better position to support himself and other family members once he finishes his studies.

Emotional Disturbance

Mindfulness Practice

How, then, can mindfulness be used as a tool to reduce pain and suffering? The solution lies with the fact that mindfulness can be used to change the relationship of an individual with his disturbing experience.

A person feels less emotionally upset when he is less disturbed by unpleasant experiences in his life. In other words, when his *relationship* to his particular form of suffering changes, he improves. But how can that happen when we all know that the mind and body react instinctively to painful experiences?

> *"If a person's basic state of mind is serene and calm, then it is possible for this inner peace to overwhelm a painful physical experience."*
>
> *— The Dalai Lama*

The answer lies with the fact that regular mindfulness practice enables the individual to become less reactive to what is happening in the moment. It is a way of staying neutral while relating to all kinds of experiences, be they positive or negative. To be mindful is to wake up, recognise and be aware of what is happening at the present moment.

For the student, instead of viewing his learning process as a battle between himself and the knowledge content, he needs to view it as a relationship. It is a relationship between him and the knowledge content.

Learning is analogous to a dance where the dancer engages with the music. It is an act of cooperation and not fighting. Many students focus on learning to get an A in their exams and school assignments, or to get praise from their teachers and parents. In many ways it is not an appropriate attention focus. If they focus on the learning process instead, it is more likely that they will enjoy and improve their performance. Likewise, the best way for the dancer to dance well is to pay attention to the dance itself while dancing instead of the likely feedback he will get from the audience.

All students have to deal with performance anxiety. A student practising mindfulness feels less anxious before the exam and recovers more quickly afterwards. If he feels stressed out in the middle of an exam, all he needs to do is to take a moment and stop working on the assessment temporarily. He looks up from the test, gets himself out of the vortex, and re-orientates himself to his exam environment. He realises that he is not facing a lion, but a school assessment. He then takes a deep breath and will be able to return to the present moment while activating his body's calming response with his breathing.

Is Mindfulness Identical to Meditation?

Most lay practitioners would choose to understand these two practices as being identical. For the more intellectually discriminative, there are certain subtle differences. A simple way to distinguish the two is to view meditation as a broader concept that includes mindfulness, but also incorporates the additional feature of an altered state of consciousness.[14]

Meditation and mindfulness have emerged from slightly different traditions. Meditation comes from a background tradition of relaxation and withdrawal from the world, whereas mindfulness comes from a background of awareness combined with attention. As such, meditation tends to refer to sit-down practice sessions during which a person tunes in to his inner calm for specific periods of time. In contrast, mindfulness can be practised at all times, throughout the day, and applied to any activity, being it eating a meal, taking a stroll in a park, feeling the freshness of the morning air, enjoying the sound of chirping birds in the trees, and, in the school context, paying attention to the teacher's words.

[14] Altered state of consciousness is different from normal waking consciousness in terms of the level of awareness, perceptions, memories, thinking, emotions and sense of time, place and self-control.

The practice of meditation has a slightly different slant from that of mindfulness. The focus of meditation tends to be more inwards on the body to give the self a deep state of relaxation. It is analogous to a diver plunging below the turbulent waves to experience the beauty of corals in the silent depths of the ocean bed. In mindfulness, however, we maintain our calmness by surfing and staying in our flow with the waves.

Contemplation, Mantra, Mudra and Prayer

The term *contemplation* is sometimes used as a substitute for meditation and mindfulness. Actually, the term refers to a train of thought about something, and the process of reflection is carried out in an alpha state. In contrast, meditation is training the mind to rest on a particular focus in a calm mental state. Mindfulness, on the other hand, uses the here and now as the mental focus. Therefore, *contemplative meditation* differs from traditional *mindfulness meditation* in that it moves the focus of attention on the breath to focusing on the reflective experience or the words being reflected upon.

The object of focus in contemplation could be an experience or a certain thought in the form of words. To help rouse the heartfelt experience of their meaning, we reflect on the words themselves and bring ideas and images to the mind to inspire the meaning. As the meaning of the words or thoughts begin to penetrate our hearts, we can often write our reflections in a narrative form. This essentially is the basis of *reflective learning,* which is discussed in the next chapter.

When meditation is combined with prayer, it may introduce confusion to some practitioners. Meditation and prayer are not identical and there are two main differences. The first is that prayer is *discursive,* and meditation is *non-discursive.* By discursive we refer to mental states that entertain multiple objects serially, and with a moving of one topic to another without order. In non-discursive states, such as in meditation, the mind entertains only a single object.

Secondly, in prayer, there is usually a recitative practice. While intense, recitative prayer requires entry into a meditative mood, the commonly practised form of mechanical repetition of a prayer script to fulfil religious obligations does not require this special mood. In addition, prayers often involve invocations and homages to deities. Meditation, however, does not involve the calling of deities. In fact, meditation seldom needs a recitative component. If it does, it is done in the form of mantras.

A *mantra* is a phrase or a series of words that are sung or chanted during a meditation. It is a linguistic device for deepening one's thought and raising the person's energy level during meditation. The word itself is derived from two words: *Man* (mind), which means "to think", and *Tra*, which means "expansion" or "to protect".

The way a mantra works is that it gives the wandering mind a focal point by producing a beat or a rhythm. In doing so, it produces a flow and makes it easier for the mind and body to grasp hold of the focus. Saying any word produces a physical vibration. The vibration so produced creates a neuro-linguistic effect and induces a sense of calmness in the person. Over time, if we know what the effect of that vibration is, then the word may come to have meaning associated with the effect of saying that word or that vibration.

Whenever the mind wanders off the meditative state, the mantra helps to bring it back. A common example is the often-used word "*Om*" in yoga meditation. It is an ancient Hindu word meaning "it is" or "to be". I recall vividly when I was in Tibet some years ago, that their local residents constantly recite the mantra "*Om mani padme hum"*[15] each time as they mindfully roll the Tibetan prayer wheel-drums stationed at various spots in the city streets of Lhasa. As another example, the World Community for Christian Meditation (WCCM) promotes the use of the mantra *"Ma-ra-na-tha"*.[16] For practical purposes, there is no necessity to know the meaning of the mantras. However, if the meaning is known to the meditating person, there is an added psycholinguistic effect. This is suitable for those who are undergoing psychotherapy and trying to overcome an addiction or start a new habit.

Sometimes, in conducting prayers, ritual gestures and group movements are introduced. The person may wish to kneel as a symbol of penance, sorrow or in adoration. He may genuflect as an act of reverence or bow as a sign of worship. In meditation, gestures are not necessary. However, if any gesture is used, it is usually single and simple, such as the *mudra*.[17]

Mudra is a Sanskrit term meaning "seal" and is a form of iconography.[18] It consists of a symbolic hand gesture

---

[15] *"Om mani padme hum"* is a Tibetan verse that supposedly contains the truth about human suffering and how to remove its root cause. *Om* means remove attachment to ego and establish generosity. *Ma* means remove attachment to jealousy and establish ethics. *Ni* means remove attachment to desire and establish patience. *Pad* means remove attachment to prejudice and establish perseverance. *Me* means remove attachment to possessiveness and establish concentration. *Hum* means remove attachment to hatred and establish wisdom.

[16] *"Maranatha"* is an Aramaic word meaning "the Lord is coming". It reminds the person to keep his eyes on eternal things of the spirit instead of dwelling on material things.

[17] Mudra is a symbolic hand position which is believed to affect the flow of energy in the body and clear the psychic centres of the mind. It is generally performed while in the sitting position during meditation.

[18] Iconography comes from Greek words meaning "image" and "to draw or write". It is the art of identifying, describing and interpreting the content of images in depicting subjects.

and has been used for thousands of years to assist in meditation. As an example, in sitting meditation the back of the right hand is commonly placed on top of the palm of the left hand, with the combination resting on the lap. Often, in yoga meditation, the tips of the thumb and index finger of each hand are placed together forming a circle, resting on the knees with the palms facing up. This gives a feeling of spaciousness and has a subtle uplifting effect on the mind.

Weaving Mindfulness into Lifestyle

The life that we live today encourages us to run from goal to goal, and from achievement to achievement, without pausing to appreciate the success. Most of our behaviour runs on autopilot. Our brain signals are directing us to adopt shortcuts and use superhighways. Our pursuit of efficiency is so intense that we relapse into old behaviours before we remember what we are supposed to do instead. We often end up not feeling satisfied with anything. At times, we even forget about the things that we have already achieved, or are privileged to have, and continue to feel empty in our lives.

Satisfaction in life is usually the result of an evaluation of the individual's life in accordance to his personal standards. It influences a person's behaviour. It is a fundamental component of his wellbeing. Wellbeing may be understood as the quest to find connectedness and transcendence[19] in life to determine what makes life worth living. It has positive effects on mental health. It helps the person to relate with himself, his values and meaning and purpose in life. It also helps him to develop optimism, and acquire hope, self-esteem and a sense of control.

---

[19] Transcendence refers to the expanding of self-boundaries towards greater awareness of one's values and dreams and the pursuit of a higher goal beyond oneself.

Life is not about being in perfection at all times. The ability to be mindful is an inherent human quality. Practising mindfulness will provide us with a tool that will keep us aware of what matters most to us and what helps us in our personal growth. As our level of mindfulness improves, our empathy, self-compassion and level of life satisfaction increase.

I have always been awed at the quality of the movie series in *Star Wars*. When I found out more about its film producer, George Lucas, I realised that he is one of those who learned to meditate from a young age and has made meditation part of his life. He taps into a desire to become more in tune with his environment and makes no distinction between his meditation practice and film work. Apparently, the movie *Star Wars* is largely based on what he has gained on his meditation journey. Yoda,[20] his screen star, is supposedly an enlightened figure on a quest for reality. George Lucas taps into a fundamental desire to become more in tune with our environment, and one of his movies in the series has a reminder for us to be mindful:

> *"A Jedi must have the deepest commitment, the most serious mind. This one a long time have I watched. All his life has he looked away ... to the future, to the horizon. Never his mind on where he was. Hmm? What he was doing."*
>
> – *The Empire Strikes Back*

Adopting a mindful lifestyle means being more kind, more self-aware and more accepting of our own thoughts and feelings. At the same time, we learn to hold our

---

[20] Yoda is a fictional character who first appeared in the film *The Empire Strikes Back* in 1980. He is a short humanoid with greenish skin colour and belongs to a mysterious species. He is a Jedi master who has tremendous power in the Force.

thoughts lightly and don't take all of them seriously. With mindfulness, we recognise our own thought patterns and learn to question any conditioned thoughts that do not serve us in our studies or our daily life.

Weaving mindfulness into our lifestyle is basically about going with the flow as we become more aware of ourselves. Life is a series of natural and spontaneous changes. Going with the flow means accepting changes without getting frustrated. It is about taking and accepting what life gives us with gratitude, without trying to mould life to be exactly what we want it to be.

We know that we cannot control everything. Yet we seem to wish that we could. We cannot change things in our mind if we are not aware of the way we think. We need to look at ourselves mindfully. Through self-observation, we will be able to take a step back as and when the situation requires it. Doing so frees us from our mental conditioning and reactive ways of thinking. As we watch our thoughts, we also listen to the voice in our head for repetitive patterns. And as we listen, we realise that there is a voice out there and that we are only listening to it. We are not our mind.

A lifestyle of mindfulness does not mean continuous moments of happiness. We will still feel our unwanted emotions, including anger, frustration, fear and sadness. However, we learn to let them come and go as part of our life. Doing so makes us more able to control our emotions. We learn to listen mindfully to our peers, classmates, friends and colleagues, and with understanding. We stop judging what they are saying. We also stop listening with the intent to reply to them. Rather, we learn to listen with the intent to understand each other.

In developing this lifestyle, we begin to accept the transient nature of things. We understand and appreciate that nothing in life is permanent. The clock ticks. Days pass by. They turn into weeks and months and eventually years. We all grow, mature and age. The water in the stream is continuously flowing. Flowers bloom and fade from existence. Air moves and becomes wind. Everything is transitory. It benefits us to remind ourselves of this constantly changing property of our life. Many of us may experience states of sadness and pain: over a failure in our exams, a relationship break-up or a parting with close friends as we leave to pursue higher studies. Some of us may have been unfortunate victims of bullying in school. We have no control over the challenges to our wellbeing, but if we can face these situations knowing that these things are not permanent, we are more likely to be able to manage them sensibly.

In acquiring inner stillness, we make a space between the things we do in our daily lives. We learn to stop multi-tasking and do one thing at a time. We take breaks before transiting to another task. We see our everyday tasks of dressing up, taking our meals, going to school, shopping and laundry not as boring, routine chores but as mindful moments. We do one thing at a time, and we do it slowly and completely. Every little routine act becomes a sacred ritual. We stop being lost in our thinking. We all have an ability to let go of our mind's compulsive chatter and access the stillness of what lies underneath.

We learn to designate time for certain tasks. We make a habit of listening to our body and mind. We discern what is nourishing and what is draining to ourselves. We treat our minds and bodies with respect and stop feeding them with junk food. We smile and serve other people while discovering that it is a great way of improving the lives of people around us. We ponder over what is necessary in our life and whether it is really that important to have all those things that are not necessary. Our urges, cravings and impulses are transformed into a wake-up call to mindfulness. We bring awareness into our desires and urges. We acknowledge our urges and allow them to be there without being caught up in the thoughts about them.

In time to come, we find our life changing. When we wake up in the morning, we ask ourselves what our intention is for the day. We consider how we might show up to our friends or colleagues to have the best impact. We ask how we might be more compassionate to others during difficult moments. We think about how we can take better care of ourselves and feel more fulfilled. Soon we will be asking what quality of the mind we want to develop. We will notice how our moods shift and how our relationships strengthen and enrich our lives.

The Gloom, The Glow

When I looked up this morning,
It was the kind of weather,
That makes you want to stay at home and hide in bed,
The gloomy sky looking down,
As the gloom hangs around everyone,
It is as if holding a mug of hot cocoa,
With small, soft, fluffy marshmallows,
Melting into the thick, rich cocoa,
Wearing comfy socks,
With a jumper and fleece leggings,
And hiding under the soft blanket,
Will take the gloom away,
And make everything better and nicer.

Just when I thought it will be a gloomy, gloomy day,
Without the comfort of my bed,
The sweetness of the fluffy marshmallow,
With the bitter aftertaste of the hot cocoa,
And the soft blanket softens the day,
There is a glow in the sky,
A glow in the midst of the gloomy sky,
My eyes light up,
If I can see myself,
I'm sure my eyes are twinkling,
And my smile is so wide,
That the gloom stays away,
The glow, the rainbow,

It's like a hope, a dream, a reassurance,
On the dark days that there will be light,
It is as if it's telling me that when things seem bleak,
And I can't see anything in front of me,
Look up and find that light, that glow, that rainbow,
Hold on to it tightly and walk towards it,

Even if it means that you'll trip, you'll stumble and fall,
Hold on to the light, stand up and keep walking,
Don't look back at the darkness behind you,
As it has passed,
Look ahead and hold your head up high,
Look up in the midst of the gloom,
Find the glow, the light, the rainbow.

By: Chong Jia Yi

Chapter Four

Mindful Learning and Teaching

Mindfulness practice in school is well known to help both students and teachers. Regular mindfulness practice trains not only our power of attention and the ability to balance our emotions. It also builds up a sense of wellbeing and promotes structural and functional changes in the brain that are associated with these experiences.

Health benefits in mindfulness are well established. These include increased immunity level, expanded capacity to manage stress, and reduced exposure to stress hormones. However, the impact of mindfulness on the education system is less often discussed.

How Mindfulness helps Students

Good health makes learning and teaching processes much easier and promotes better performance on the part of both teachers and students. It helps students to foster self-regulation skills for academic achievement and emotional wellbeing. By self-regulation I am referring to the ability of the student to control his behaviour, emotions or thoughts and change them in accordance with the requirements of the educational setting.

Mindfulness supports the student's readiness to learn in addition to strengthening his attention and concentration. Through a self-calming technique, the student is more able to self-reflect and develop greater self-awareness of his own abilities, talents and potential.

The self-calming effect also reduces his anxiety before examinations. It improves classroom participation by supporting impulse control. In itself, mindfulness is a tool for stress reduction and for enhancing social and emotional learning. In turn, this fosters healthy relationships with his peers. All these lead to not only individual wellbeing but also to the development of a holistic education culture and environment, which will be discussed in Chapter 6.

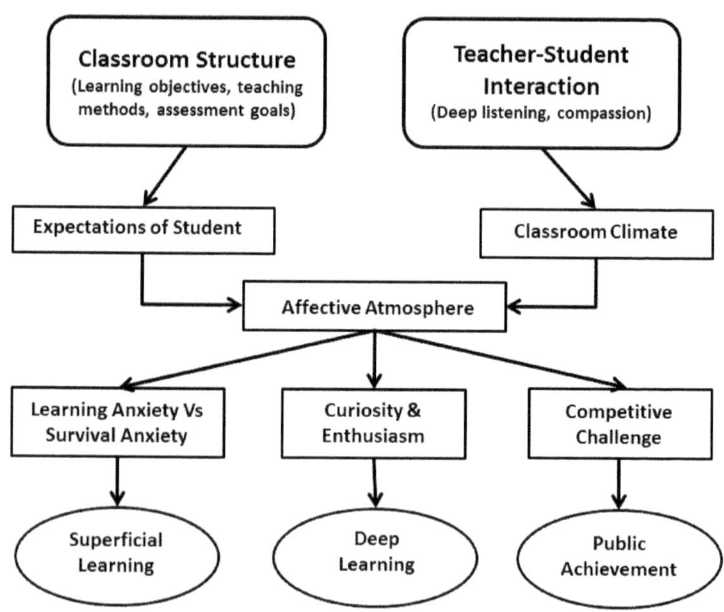

Being Mindful of the Learning Approach

It is not uncommon for students to take a *superficial learning* approach, especially when they see learning as a means towards some other end. Pleasing their parents or aiming for a better job are common goals. Students with a superficial approach would simply regard the learning task as a demand to be met. They would, during lesson time, simply focus on the actual words used by the teacher on the subject matter rather than on their meaning. They tend to see the components of the learning tasks as discrete and unrelated to each other. They also prefer to rely on memorisation of these components to complete their lesson. They are not mindful of the personal meanings that these tasks may have on them. Part of the reason is that they are often resentful of the amount of time taken to learn the subject matter and are worried about failing exams if they are slower than their peers.

In contrast, students who are mindful of the intrinsic interest in the subject matter tend to be able to achieve *deep learning*. They focus on the meaning of the subject matter and see the learning task as personally involving. They are also able to integrate task components with each other.

Learning of any kind requires attentive listening and the fluent use of words. Mindfulness guards the senses. It endows the person with circumspection and dignity and disallows the senses to play with the tantalising joys of the world. By recollecting awareness into the present and remembering his actions as appropriate and purposeful in time and place, mindfulness trains the student's attention to thoughts, words and experiences. This practice is particularly beneficial in children with attention deficits. On the other hand, mindless learning occurs when rules and routines govern behaviour and compromise the quality of a student's education.

True education has the aim of awakening the student to the world. To bring mindfulness to the classroom, several factors in addition to attention and concentration are important. These include joy, curiosity, equanimity and diligence. Teachers who have introduced mindfulness to schools notice that those students who benefit most from mindfulness are those with short attention span and a poor ability to focus on any one activity for long. These students tend to become calmer in the classroom and less reactive to emotional situations. As a result, they have a greater ability to focus on the present moment and their learning experience.

Some of the additional techniques used for bringing mindfulness to the classroom include focusing on posture, breathing, visualisation and attention. Posture is important because it sets up the body in a state of relaxed concentration. Breath meditation is a good preparation for activities like brainstorming and free writing. Attention, as discussed previously, is useful for stilling the mind whereas visualisation acts as the brain's "inner eye".

Mindfulness and Reflective Learning

Mindfulness enriches reflective learning. The pursuit of self-awareness in mindfulness leads to an exploration of our own thoughts and emotions in everyday life, particularly in one-to-one interactions and relationships with others. Reflective learning occurs when a student explores an experience in which he has to identify the nature of his role in that experience. This includes his thinking, emotions and behaviour. The purpose of the reflection is to understand what he and others have contributed to the situation and outcomes, so that he can improve his contribution and the outcome in future situations.

When students are mindful, they become more aware of their environment, thoughts, actions and emotions. This prepares them for reflective learning. They are more tuned to their body senses: their sight, touch, hearing, smell and taste. Hence, they are more perceptive as a result. They also have a clearer perception of their role in the planning of their assignments.

When students are exploring an experience where they have to identify what happened and what their role in the experience was, mindfulness helps. They will be able to better notice and recall what transpired when they planned and took action. They get a clearer perception of why those consequences came about. This is often relevant to school outings, excursions and outdoor learning. The student allows himself to experience surprise and puzzlement when he encounters a unique situation or an uncertain environment. Thereafter he reflects on the phenomenon before him and uses it as part of his creative writing. An example of mindful learning will be presented in the next chapter.

Mindfulness in Group Learning

Reflective learning frequently involves learning in a group. In this situation socio-emotional learning forms an important part. When students improve in their socio-emotional learning, they become more cognisant and understanding in their relationships towards their peers and are able to show more empathy to each other.

In group learning the student is often exposed to "supportive challenge" from his peers. There are two dimensions of learning when fellow students challenge each other's perspectives and assumptions – an *intrapersonal* and an *interpersonal*. These two dimensions reinforce and build on each other. Mindfulness practice enhances both these dimensions.

In a group discussion, it is expected that group members will have differing opinions and perspectives. If the discussion is devoid of conflict it is likely that the participants are not sharing their opinions. In managing such group conflicts, the key is for the discussion leader to manage the participants' emotions, so that they can improve their objectivity in the moment, listen effectively and avoid knee-jerk emotional reactions. The use of diaphragmatic breathing to keep focused on the goal and keep calm is important. Be mindful of introverts. There will be some who do not speak up in a group or have difficulty getting a word in. In such situations the group facilitator needs to be mindful of creating an opening for them.

How Mindfulness Helps Teachers

Teaching is a very stressful occupation. Most schoolteachers are overworked. Apart from teaching responsibilities, standards, curriculum and examination requirements are constantly increasing and there is no time for them to care for themselves. All too often, they are struggling to avoid burn-out, and self-care is needed. As they engage their minds and hearts to provide support for students who are also struggling, they learn about the sorrow and pain that their students experience. As such, there is a risk that they extend the students' anxiety and trauma to themselves.

Mindfulness practice helps teachers in two areas. Firstly, it improves the teacher's responsiveness to student needs. This is often made possible through the skill of being observant in the moment in combination with effective listening.

It is common to find inexperienced teachers who are judgmental of their own teaching style and practice. Their minds are clouded with uncertainties. "Will I be able to deliver the content effectively in this class? Are the students actually benefiting from my lesson? What happens if they don't?"

Often the act of judging themselves distracts them from connecting with the awareness of the students' behaviour. Awareness enables them to respond to student needs effectively rather than reacting in each moment in the classroom. By reflecting on the students' behaviour and being mindful of how the teaching is being conducted, it is easier to make teaching more creative. When students are interested in the teaching, they are more engaged in their learning, with less tendency to misbehave.

Secondly, mindfulness helps the teacher to enhance the classroom climate and supports healthy relationships in school. This is often done through the development of compassion and empathy. Through mindfulness teachers can observe the tension in their own body during lessons and be aware of the discrepancy between their personal philosophy of teaching and how they are actually teaching. With a relaxed mind and body, they are ready to take on whatever happens next in the classroom. If they are worried about something, they can actually reflect on why they are worried and look at their perceptions of the situation.

Secondary school and college teachers are known to complain about a high level of stress in their teaching duties and responsibilities. Each time they walk into a class they seldom know what student behaviour they will encounter. Yet, what lies in front of them is a space for learning and growth for themselves. They learn to discern when *not* to advise or speak. This involves mindful listening skills. Their ability to listen and to set aside their compulsion to share what is on their mind reveals their willingness to trust the presence of the spirit of learning in the environment.

Deep Listening

In our fast-paced society, one of the best gifts that teachers can offer to their students is a listening heart. To be able to listen mindfully to the student is to carve a safe and sacred space for the student to face the mystery of suffering in the education process. Not infrequently, it is a journey of courage and it requires preparation on the teacher's part. For listening to be effective, the teacher needs a contemplative mind that is open, alert, attentive, calm and receptive.

Unsatisfying communication is rampant in our society. This includes student-teacher relationships. Mindful listening on the part of the teacher with his committed cultivation of self-awareness and compassion is the key to changing this social habit.

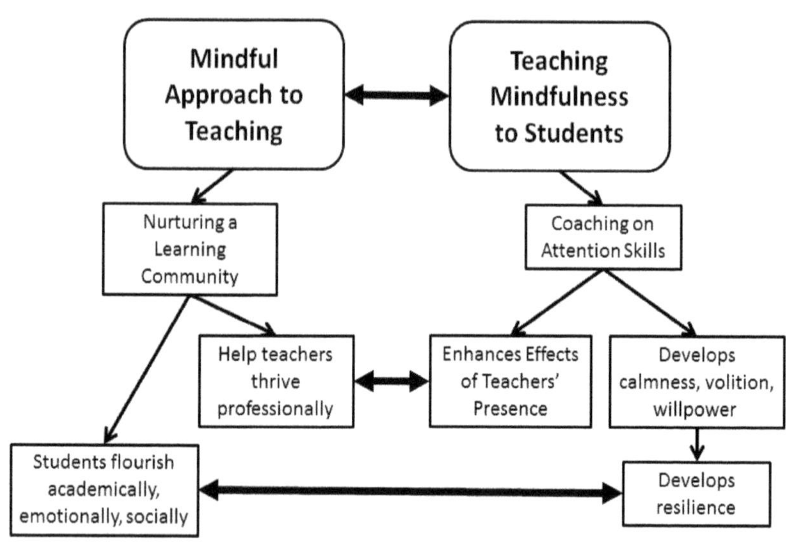

Mindful listening is a way of hearing in which we are fully present with what is happening in the moment without trying to judge the situation. We let go of our inner clamouring and usual assumptions. Instead, we listen precisely to what is being said, in order to understand the problem being presented. However, this isn't easy. In conversation we tend to be so focused on projecting our opinions and preparing our replies that we often fail to hear the messages of others.

Mindful listening changes the way we normally engage in a dialogue. This form of listening is reliant on a commitment to self-control and self-awareness. Listening mindfully invites the teacher to put the student at the centre and create a better relationship with his students in the process. Teachers skilled in listening tend to experience more joy and peace in their career. They learn rich and precious lessons about other human beings and, in the process, about themselves as humans.

Beyond mindful listening, the teacher develops deep listening where he not only hears what is being said but seeks to understand the person behind the student's words. He listens between the lines and watches the body language. He hears the student's emotion, detects his needs and perceives his values. The goal of deep listening is to hear beyond the words to grasp the essence of what the words and feelings are pointing to.

Deep listening is not just mindful listening. It is also a form of holistic practice because it unites the mind and the heart. It occurs when the mind is quiet. It is like listening to our favourite music, the sound of a stream rushing by, or a bird singing. When we listen to these delightful sounds we are under no pressure. We are not analysing or figuring out what we are listening to. We are simply letting the feelings and sounds influence us.

Deep listening is not about struggling to interpret. It is purely a receptive state of mind. When the teacher listens deeply, he lets go of any beliefs about the student and any past memories or prejudices of him. He focuses first and foremost on his self-awareness in order to better communicate with his students. Without a clear idea of his relationship with himself, he cannot improve his relationship with his students. In fact, deep listening requires letting go of the *Story of Self.* This letting go is the first step towards perceiving and hearing others more fully.

Deep listening is contemplative in quality. It is active listening that calls on a special quality of attention. It involves listening from a caring place in ourselves to deeper and subtler levels of meaning in the other person. It is a type of listening that is empathic, supportive and trusting. It encompasses the practice of suspending self-oriented, reactive thinking and opening our awareness to the unknown and unexpected.

Resilience and Mindfulness

A student who has performed inadequately in his examinations often has to deal with the reality of falling short of his own or his parents' expectations. However, when he chooses to adopt a fear-based survival framework to view his situation, problems arise. He may react to the situation with negative thoughts such as: "I am a failure; I have brought shame to my family" or "I'll never get into university at this rate". The fear embedded in such reactions determines his reality and locks him in shame, powerlessness and blame. Depending on his coping ability and level of maturity, he may lapse into anxiety, depression and, at his worst, embrace suicidal thoughts. All these emotional states are counterproductive to effective learning.

Effective learning in the school environment requires attention, organisation, comprehension, memory, trust and relationships. A student who has experienced trauma or abuse from his early childhood often finds his ability to form relationships undermined. He will then have difficulty regulating his emotions and learning the necessary cognitive skills to succeed in his academic performance. The way to counterbalance trauma is to seek healing and build a capacity to rebound from stress. This capacity is known as resilience. In this situation, mindfulness is a key factor.

Neuroscience studies have clearly shown that mindfulness meditation supports the development of a person's ability to rebound from stress. Mindful people are observed to be able to cope better with difficult thoughts and emotions without being overwhelmed. What mindfulness practice does is to weaken the chain of associations that make people obsessed about their failures.

Every day in school the teacher will find students who are feeling tired, frustrated, alone and possibly anxious. Some may be struggling with a learning disability while others are coping with poor family relationships and are in danger of dropping out of school. To foster resiliency and hope, the teacher must provide unconditional love and positive regard in a safe and caring environment.

A safe environment is one that has a friendly setting where the child feels respected, valued and encouraged to reach his full potential. The teacher must value and embrace the opinions and views of school children and young people. This is where the teaching of mindfulness meditation in school is relevant for both teachers and students. It helps to cultivate the necessary empathy and compassion in the educational environment.

The range of stressful situations encountered by young people includes the areas of study, family situations, romantic relationships and emotional wellbeing. There are various strategies that schools can use for enhancing resilience, chief of which is the promotion of a positive teacher-student relationship and peer-to-peer relationships. A sense of connectedness and belonging to the school protects these young people through building their resilience. The skills of self-awareness, social awareness, compassion and creative thinking lie at the heart of personal relationships and are pre-requisites for fostering resiliency.

Compassion and Resilience

Compassion is about recognising suffering with a feeling of empathy and respect for the person who is stricken by misfortune. Whenever we notice that we are moved by another person's suffering we are actually being compassionate. This is often associated with the desire to help to alleviate it. For instance, a student who is on his way to school and walks past a homeless man at the roadside begging for change may want to pause for a moment to consider how difficult life could have been for the beggar. Rather than ignoring him, the student may be touched and feel the urge to help him in some way. Compassion therefore entails feelings of kindness and understanding others who are in pain. Being mindful of these feelings paves the way for the desire to ameliorate suffering to emerge naturally.

Empathy comes hand in hand with compassion. To develop empathy, we need to be in tune with the feelings and needs of others. However, compassion goes beyond that. We are compassionate when we act on those feelings by helping, soothing and caring for others in protective ways. Students who are struggling with trauma would therefore need compassionate teachers to help them develop resilience. It is worth noting that some teachers themselves are barely coping and cannot bounce back from the challenges they themselves face. As such, they would not have the strength to promote resiliency among their students. For them self-compassion is needed.

Self-compassion is simply about turning compassion inwards. It involves being warm, kind and understanding towards ourselves when we fail, feel inadequate or are struggling with misery. Instead of criticising ourselves for our weakness, we need to recognise that imperfection and difficulties are an inevitable part of life. We need to soothe ourselves whenever we are in pain and learn to nurture ourselves instead of getting angry when we fall short of expectations. In acknowledging and accepting our own shortcomings without judgment, we turn our attention to do what is necessary to help ourselves.

Whenever we pass harsh judgment on ourselves, we tend to feel isolated. By highlighting something we don't like about ourselves, we tend to feel that everyone else is perfect and we are the only one that falls short of ideal. Distorted thinking is not uncommon. The student might think that things always go wrong with his preparation for school exams; that his scores are always disappointing; and that his peers always seem to have an easier time and are able to sail through their studies. This common form of distorted thinking is rather harmful. It focuses us on our inadequacy to the extent that we ignore everything else except the worthless part of ourselves. When things go wrong, we often go into a problem-solving mode without recognising the need to comfort ourselves for the difficulties we are facing.

There is a real danger of over-identifying ourselves with negative thoughts and feelings associated with our inadequacies and failures. We tend to exaggerate the implication of our self-worth. Being mindful to our difficult feelings will help us to gain clarity and emotional neutrality to both the educational and life difficulties we face. When a student is mindful, a non-judgmental state of mind will help him to observe his thoughts and feelings as they are, without denying or reacting to them.

A frequent mistake made by many students is the belief that self-criticism is necessary to motivate themselves. They fail to realise that the motivation derived from self-criticism arises from fear whereas the motivation that one gets from self-compassion arises from love of oneself. To the extent that self-criticism does have some motivational property, it is because we tend to be driven by the desire to avoid self-judgment when we fail. It is a way of shaming ourselves into action when we are confronted with our own weakness. The truth is that constant criticism makes us feel worthless and depressed. Self-criticism is a known cause for anxiety and depression. When the student knows that failure will be met with a barrage of self-criticism, it can become too frightening for him to even try. This results in procrastination and under-achievement.

With self-compassion, the student is kind to himself, especially during his own moments of suffering. He strives to achieve, to take on challenging tasks and to learn new skills. He obtains more clarity about his feelings, ruminates less and copes better with adversities. His feelings of social connectedness and improved relationships give him a more meaningful sense of life. This is not associated with the level of educational performance standards he sets for himself. He aims as high as all competitive students do, but he will accept that he cannot always reach his goals.

In developing compassion through mindfulness, what we practise becomes stronger with constant repetition. It is like developing our own highway. When we are hurried and stressed, we tend to lose touch with our own natural compassion. Mindfulness helps us to slow down and see things more clearly. Let us take an example. A group of students is being told to hurry and run to a particular venue to be in time to attend an important lecture, and one student in the group falls down in the process. The rest of the group will tend to leave him alone to get up and reach the lecture hall by himself. In contrast, if the students had ample time to prepare themselves, they would be more likely to pause, help him get up and examine his injury first.

Another way in which mindfulness helps to develop compassion is that it enables us to see our interdependence. When we see clearly that we are not separate or independent of each other, compassion naturally arises. To illustrate this, Jon Kabat-Zinn uses the metaphor of the right hand extracting a splinter embedded in the left hand and the left hand feeling so thankful about the gracious act.

Mindfulness helps us to remember our essential nature and we learn to welcome all our past experiences with compassion, even though some may be seemingly unforgiveable. In fact, the meditating practitioners from the Tibetan tradition would highlight that the beneficial effects of mindfulness on health, memory and cognitive skills are secondary effects. The primary purpose of calming the mind and heightening attention is to attain a form of enlightenment that would lead to a deep abiding compassion.

The Suffering Student

All sufferings are a result of a changed relationship of an individual with his disturbing experience. A student will feel less emotionally painful when he is less disturbed by the unpleasant experiences of poor performance in exams or a failed romantic relationship. In other words, when his *relationship* to his particular form of suffering changes, he improves. But how can that happen when we all know that the mind and body react instinctively to painful experiences?

The answer lies again with practising mindfulness. We develop a skill that enables us to be less reactive to what is happening in the moment. It is a way of relating ourselves more effectively to all experiences, be they positive or negative. To be mindful is to wake up, recognise and be aware of what is happening at the present moment. It helps us to get to the opposite state when we are being caught up with distracting thoughts and opinions of what is happening at the present moment.

Students who believe that they are suffering are often those who are preoccupied with past or future events. There are those who feel regret, sadness or guilt over failures and past trauma, while people who are anxious will fear the future. Their suffering increases by straying away from the present moment. As we get absorbed with the mental activity and feelings of an unpleasant past event, we begin to daydream and may get into a self-pity mode. In this situation, we often feel as if we are stuck with watching the movie of our lives. Mindfulness helps us to step out of our conditioned mind and see things as they actually are, and not what we are ruminating about.

Building Resilience

Resilience is the ability to bounce back from adversity. There are four areas in our life that we must understand before we can help ourselves to build our resilience. Mindfulness has a role in all of them.

The first area is that of self-confidence. We all have strengths and we need a good understanding of our strengths and capacity to cope in order to create a bedrock of comfort that will enable us to deal with life challenges. This is basically an issue of building self-awareness, and mindfulness is at the heart of it. Confidence is built on positive emotions and mindfulness helps to cultivate it. This involves not only confidence in our accomplishments and abilities but also how comfortable we are in dealing with others, particularly those whom we do not know very well.

The second area is that of social support. Students who have supportive families and peers choose more active coping strategies for dealing with stress situations. It opens up additional resources in terms of mental input and practical help. Often teachers and family members can give support in terms of providing information, advice and different perspectives about a situation of concern. Advising a student how to approach a subject or a task can make all the difference for him. The role of mindfulness is particularly relevant in that it helps the individual to enhance his social connection with others and builds his self-esteem. Esteem support is particularly important for students. When teachers and parents show encouragement and respect by praising the student's achievement, it helps him to build confidence in himself.

The third area is about adaptability. This is crucial in dealing with ambiguity, uncertainty and change. For example, the transition from high school to university is a very stressful developmental period for most students. It is associated with a lot of personal, social and emotional difficulties. However, adaptability allows us to perceive the transition as an opportunity rather than a threat. We need to learn how to react with appropriate and proper urgency in crisis situations. We need to remain composed and cool when faced with difficult circumstances such as a highly demanding study load. We can learn not to overreact to unexpected situations. We think outside the given parameters to see if there is a more effective approach to resolve an issue. It is now known that mindfulness practice alters certain parts of the brain and changes the manner in which the neural networks connect with each other.[21] These changes improve cognitive flexibility, which contributes to better adaptability.

Adaptability allows us to adjust to different situations and think through the consequences in a logical way. Quite often we need to take effective action without knowing the total picture and we need to be ready to change gear in response to unexpected events.

---

[21] "Mindfulness can literally change your brain" by Christina Congleton, Britta K. Hözel, Sara W. Lazar. *Harvard Business Review.* https://hbr.org/2015/01/mindfulness-can-literally-change-your-brain

Mindfulness calms our mind so that we do not subject ourselves to the negative impact of the fight-or-flight response.[22] Mindfulness practice also opens up our mind to new possibilities and options which we may otherwise miss or overlook in the heat of our adrenaline release. The ability to consider an alternative scenario can help us to reframe challenges such that they reduce their negative pressure on us.

The fourth area is that of a life purpose. The sense of purpose is important for resilience because it helps us to put things into perspective when things become difficult. It keeps us and our life on track in the right direction. We know that whatever decision we make in the face of the challenges will ultimately align with our life goal. On a day-to-day level, it is equally important to find a sense of purpose in our studies. We need to identify with the goals and objectives of what we study in school and how the acquired content knowledge aligns with our life purpose.

A strong sense of purpose can help us find meaning in the face of adverse situations. The practice of mindfulness helps us to acknowledge the fleeting processes of the mind as just thoughts and feelings which we can let go. That stops the superficial thinking from influencing the bigger and deeper decisions we make about our lives. In turn, this allows us to start living the life that we have always meant to lead. If we have a strong sense of life purpose, it will provide us with an anchor to hold on to when our life gets difficult.

---

[22] Fight-or-flight response is an acute physiological reaction occurring in response to a perceived attack, harmful event or survival scenario. It is brought about by a release of hormones from the medulla of the adrenal gland of the body.

Journey of Learning

To be with yourself on this journey,
To learn,
To understand,
To listen,
To think,
To interpret,
To be searching the meaning of life,
Of love,
Of breathing,
Of being yourself,
It's a full circle you're chasing,
For we can never stop seeking,
For each time you know a little more than before,
You're back
To the circle with ourselves.

By: Chong Jia Yi

Chapter Five

Contemplative Learning and Mindfulness

Application of mindfulness to the learning environment is closely related to the concept of *contemplative education.* This concept refers to a set of pedagogical practices designed to cultivate the potential of mindful awareness in a context in which the values of personal growth, moral living and caring for others are also nurtured. This deviates from mainstream education, which is more focused on knowledge acquisition, skills development and personal achievement, and driven by the materialistic culture we live in.

Contemplative Education

The essence of contemplative education resides in its emphasis on holism[23] or wholesomeness. This form of education integrates introspective and experiential learning into academic studies. It invites students to become more aware of their inner world. It connects their learning to their own values and sense of meaning, following which they would be able to apply their first-

[23] The word "holistic" means considering all the parts of something as a cohesive whole. In humans it refers to the wholesome state of the individual in which all four dimensions, the physical, mental, emotional and spiritual perspectives, are balanced. While the word "wholistic" would make more sense, "holistic" is the only accepted spelling.

person experiences to what they are learning in the classroom. This practice increases the students' attention and decreases stress. It also gives a deeper meaning to a tertiary education through self-knowledge. This enables them to form richer, deeper relationships with their peers, communities and the world around them. We can simply describe this as *interconnectedness.*

Contemplative education equips the student with perspectives and techniques that bring forth their own way of connecting their hearts and minds. Through its quality of interconnectedness and the cultivation of conscious awareness, it fosters personal growth and social transformation. It is a form of learning that is infused with insight and compassion for him and others and is honed through the practice of meditation. In contemplative education, the learning process goes beyond the traditional mode of *transmission learning,* which emphasises lectures and drill. It includes inquiry and problem solving, known as *transactional learning,* and self-discovery, which is also called *transformational learning*.

In essence, the concept of contemplative education integrates contemplative practices, contemplative philosophy and contemplative orientation into an educational setting that helps to develop wholeness in the student and teacher. At the heart of the concept is a blend of mindfulness and awareness. It emphasises direct learning, moment by moment, and focuses on the integration of thoughts, sensations, emotions and the synchronisation of mind and body.

Narratives are an excellent way of representing and understanding our contemplative experience. Increasingly, educators are beginning to rely more on narrative inquiry[24] as a means of moving beyond brooding and intellectual analysis to the gaining of insights. The art of verbally illustrating the interpretation of a situation has been found to be a very powerful way of learning. People often tell stories to help to make sense of and organise their lives. In fact, storytelling has been integral to the way that human beings learn even before recorded history. For many generations ancient peoples have huddled around campfires to share their knowledge and experiences and express their culture and identities.

A Contemplative Learning Experience

While I was writing this book, I decided to take a break and embark on a personal, contemplative learning journey. The goal was to allow myself to experience once again the impact of *everyday mindfulness* on my learning process. For this purpose, I decided on a summer holiday in the Hubei province in central-eastern China. This is an area that has become widely known recently when it was the epicentre of a massive coronavirus outbreak that turned into a pandemic.

Historically, the Hubei province has a rich culture and is well known as the region where the military battles, plots, struggles and intrigues of the feudal lords of the Warring States, better known as the *Three Kingdoms*,[25] which took place during the turbulent end of the Han Dynasty.

After exploring various learning options, I decided on a trip to explore the legendary forest mountains of

---

[24] Narrative inquiry is the study of experience understood narratively. It is a methodology of gathering information for the process of research through the tool of storytelling.

[25] *Romance of the Three Kingdoms* is a 14th-century historical novel set in the years 169–280 AD. It is one of the four great classics of Chinese literature and its influence on Asia is comparable with that of Shakespeare on English literature.

Shennongjia (⍰⍰⍰), which I used to read about as a child. I was aware that a beautiful nature reserve exists in that region, making it valuable as a learning resource.

As a tourist spot, Shennongjia is reputed for being a habitat for the golden snub-nosed monkey and the Chinese giant salamander. For the nature lover, the site is better known for being a protective ground for the largest primary forests remaining in central China. I was attracted to this fact as I strongly wanted to mindfully experience a primitive environment in nature, having been a city dweller for most of my life.

The name Shennong (⍰⍰) comes from the history of a legendary Chinese emperor and ancestor of the nation in remote antiquity. He is believed to have been a herbalist who explored the mountains in that region in search of various medicinal herbs to treat the sicknesses of the local residents and his countrymen. The word *jia* (⍰) refers to the ladder or lattice wooden structure that he used to facilitate the picking of plants from the mountain slopes that were rich in herbal value. The thought of the trip was exciting in itself as it sounded like a practical lesson in exploring traces of a Chinese mythology.

I made the trip to the destination in stages. I flew to Wuhan (武汉), the hot, dry capital city of Hubei province. The first part of the trip was a five-hour coach journey from Wuhan to the adjacent city of Yichang (宜昌). The latter was located very near the famous Three Gorges Dam (三峡大坝), which is reputed to be the world's largest hydroelectric power project.

The remaining part of the coach journey from Yichang to the foot of the Shennongjia mountains took another three and a half hours. As I looked through the coach's window admiring the countryside scenery, I was amazed that the coach was travelling on a special highway, known as the water-highway (水上公路) to the local residents. This highway was built on top of a river valley using tall concrete H-shaped stilt supports. I decided to take a short break and got down from the coach to observe the awesome engineering structure.

Apparently, the water-highway is something which the local residents were very proud of. I soon understood the reason. Viewed from a distance, the highway has the orientation and shape of a dragon, which is a strong symbol of Chinese culture. Chinese dragons are a symbol of strength, power and good luck. They supposedly have potent auspicious powers and control over rain, floods and hurricane. Historically, for many dynasties, the dragon has been a symbol of the Chinese emperor, and the imperial throne has always been called the Dragon Throne.

I stared at the magnificent engineering structure for several minutes. The design is a commendable feat. It struck me that the enormous efforts behind the highway project also reflected the mindfulness of the local government in preserving the natural environment. The alternative to constructing the highway was to build roads and tunnels on the mountain slopes in the conventional way. However, that would have caused excessive damage to the virgin forests and the natural environment.

The coach eventually stopped at the foot of the Shennongjia mountains. For a moment I felt excited, as I was getting ready myself for the ascent and an adventurous trip. Next to the entrance gate to the nature reserve were some stalls manned by the local residents and a few rows of eateries that served hot meals to travellers coming from other cities. I did not pause to look at them. Instead I lost no time in starting my long-awaited excursion.

I went past the entrance gate with my mind set on conquering the mountainous heights. I treated the journey upwards as an exercise in *everyday mindfulness.* With each step forward, I focused my awareness on lifting my foot, bending my knees, and letting my soles take a grip on the stone slabs mindfully as I steadily moved myself up the stairway on the mountain slope.

The ascent turned out to be slower than I expected. The slope was steep and the steps narrow. I came across several waterfalls on my way up. I paused for several moments to scrutinise each one of them. There was a sense of joy in listening to the sound of water splashing on the rocks. I was aware that I had to be mindful of my grip on those steps that were wet and slippery because of the waterfall.

I looked closely at the physical formation of the waterfalls. Each of them was about three to five metres in height. It was calming as I watched the water splashing down in a cascaded manner and bouncing off the rocks quickly. As the dense white-coloured water falls from the cliff, I observed how the droplets fanned out and dropped vertically downwards, thinning out to a faint, greyish colour. All of a sudden, I was being reminded that the spectacular landform had been created by an ongoing erosion process of nature.

What I learned from my Geography lessons in my schooldays became clearer now. Waterfalls form at the upper part of a river where vertical erosion takes place. Two layers of different types and densities of rock are necessary for its formation. There is a top layer of hard rock such as granite, which is more resistant to erosion, and a bottom layer of softer rock such as sandstone, which is more prone to rapid erosion. The water passes over this area and the soft rock erodes at a faster pace than the hard rock, which gradually forms a step and a notch at the riverbed. The hydraulic action from the falling water gives rise to further erosion at both the plunge pool and the notch. As the notch grows there is insufficient support from the hard rock to hold the water and the overhang breaks off and falls into the plunge pool as smaller pieces of rock. This acts on the plunge pool and the force of corrosion contributes to the waterfall formation. The process repeats itself over time and gradually the waterfall retreats upstream as the notch and plunge pool are further eroded. This eventually leads to the formation of a steep gorge.

As I continued my ascent, I felt sprinkles of tiny water droplets on my face splashing from the plunge pools. As the waterfall roared and rumbled as it wound around the rocks, I sensed that the air was crisp and fresh. It came to mind that the smell of freshness is somewhat similar to what we often experience after a heavy rain. I then recalled the chemistry of air freshness. The fresh smell has been attributed to an oil emitted by certain plants during dry periods whereupon it is absorbed by soil and rocks. It is then released into the air together with another compound called *geosmin*, a product of certain bacteria, and which is emitted by wet soil. It is also recognised that the human nose is very sensitive to the fragrant scent of geosmin.

In contrast, there was a musty odour emanating from the surrounding trees and rocks. I noticed many of the rocks next to the waterfalls were covered with layers of green moss, giving the impression of uneven patches of pasture. It was as if the moss was conveying a special meaning to me. I paused for a moment and reflected. I noticed that the moss was thriving in places that the sun did not reach. A message came to my mind: "It is important that as individuals we need to thrive even when we are left alone or kept out of the social spotlight."

I continued with my trip up. Halfway up the long flight of stairs was a welcome gate structure. It was made up of wooden logs with the words "Ba Tribe" (巴人部落)written on a wooden banner. The words were in Chinese seal script. The seal script is an ancient form of Chinese characters that appeared during the Qin Dynasty, 221 BC. It is believed to be the first Chinese script and it evolved from oracle bone script. It takes the form of pictograms and ideographs. Today, it is only used in seals or name chops.

The Ba people are an ethnic group that live in Eastern Sichuan and Western Hubei provinces in ancient China. As far as I was aware, they flourished during the period 1600–700 BC but mysteriously declined and disappeared during the Warring States period (475–221 BC). This left behind many riddles as to their origin and whereabouts of the remains of their civilisation.

I stared at the panel for a few moments and several questions came to mind. "Were the Ba people the original aboriginal inhabitants of the Three Gorges area?" I would have expected them to be so. "Where are their descendants today, especially since they had a powerful kingdom at one time? Where also are the mausoleums of their Ba kings located?" When I searched the history texts later after the trip, I found no definite answers.

Next, I noticed five bovine skulls were attached to the wooden frame of the log gate. One skull, in particular, was sitting sternly on top of the wooden banner. I stared at the skulls for a minute and wondered if they carried any special symbolism for the Ba people. "Does the bovine skull represent life-long protection from natural elements? Does it symbolise, courage, strength, toughness and durability like it does for South American natives?" Interestingly, I recalled that it is also a symbol for Taurus, the second zodiac sign in Western astrology which describes the same qualities.

I went past the gate, continued my journey uphill and decided to perform an exercise in *mindful walking.*

Walking Meditation

Mindful walking is a form of walking meditation. There are several phases in the walking exercise where we can develop mindfulness. The nature of the primary and secondary objects of meditation has been explained in Chapter 2. In this situation, the experiences of the foot during a walking exercise can be a *primary object* of a meditative experience. In mindful walking we allow our awareness to focus on the sense of stepping on the ground. We follow one foot at a time. We focus on the moving foot regardless of whether or not the stationary foot produces a stronger sensation.

In raising our heel, we feel the increasing pressure on the front end of the longitudinal arch of the foot and the under-surface of the toes. As we raise the foot off the ground, we notice the contraction of the thigh muscles above the knee. We concentrate on the feeling of the lifting action of the knee while the foot is being raised and moved some distance in front. Next we are mindful of the dropping action of the leg as we tread on the next step and press the foot down.

Apart from the foot, all other meditation objects are treated as *secondary objects* in mindful walking. Movement of the foot strengthens our awareness and is equally accessible as a primary object as the breath in a sitting meditation. When we stay mindful with the moving foot, all the secondary objects are naturally noticed as we walk.

Totem Pole

Next, after a long flight of steps, I arrived at a stop and resting station at the mountain waist where I saw a cluster of four totem poles. Totem poles are hand-carved monuments created by the indigenous people. They are generally created to represent ancestry, history, lineage or mythological figures of the tribal people. In the West, totem poles represent important stories and events and are well known among the native tribes of northwest America. Less well known is the fact that they are also a common feature among the minority tribes in China. I paused to examine the images being on the poles to see if and how they were different from those of the West. Interestingly, on the poles were carved pictures of the dragon, symbols of the bull head, primitive people, plants with some ancient Chinese characters.

Many people might have mistaken the totem poles as objects of religious worship. The truth is that they are not meant to be. Rather, they represent the cultural pride and kinship of the Ba people. The totems were meant to be revered and not worshipped. Although the early Chinese people had their gods, these totems were not on the god level. It then came to mind for me to reflect on the belief system to which the totems belong, and how it differs from those of the Pacific Northwest.

In general, the indigenous tribes in China had a great reverence for nature and they believed that they lived at the same existential level as animals and plants. Each life form had positive characteristics for them to emulate. Each tribal group would identify with a few animals and plants and attempt to follow the positive characteristics of these animals or plants in their daily lives. Instead of treating them as objects for worship, they were regarded as objects of reverence. These animal and plant objects were not on the same level as the gods they believed in. It is remarkable therefore that the Chinese people spend so much time and energy in creating the huge totems.

I stared at the dragon of the totem poles and several thoughts came to mind. The question arose as to whether the tie-ins between this belief system of the ancient Chinese and that of the Native American tribes could be a coincidence?

From what I recall from my schooldays, the Chinese dragon differs significantly from the Western dragon in symbolism. In the West, the English word dragon has its origin in the Greek word *drakon*, which means serpent. In English mythology, a dragon lived in a pond and poisoned the countryside. It induced the villagers to offer sacrifices of sheep and human beings to save themselves but was ultimately killed by St George. In Greek mythology, the dragon appeared in different forms. As Typhon, it was supposedly a monstrous dragon with one hundred heads of a snake, ultimately defeated by Zeus. As Python it was an earth-dragon that guarded the Delphic oracle and was killed by Apollo. The Lernaean Hydra is a water serpent with many heads that was slain by Heracles. All these brought to mind that the Western dragon is a symbol of evil and considered a fierce, violent, greedy and cruel animal.

In contrast, the Chinese dragon is a totem of the Chinese nation itself. It ranks on the highest level among all animals and is deified by and considered sacred to the Chinese people. It is usually depicted as an image of a snake-like creature with eagle claws, scales of fish and antlers of a deer. It lives in water and has control over thunder, lightning and clouds. It floats in the air and swims in water. It is perceived to be a benevolent creature that helps to solve difficulties and protects human beings from disasters. It carries symbolic meanings of fortune, good luck, peace and authority. It is associated with courage and strength of the individual. The dragon totem brings magic into life and helps the person to view the world through the eyes of mystery and wonder.

Shennong Forest

I continued with my ascent and, after several hundred steps, I finally arrived at the Shennong Forest. This part of the nature reserve has been renovated and newly named as the *Shennong Merit and Virtue Forest* to attract visitors. I saw an explanatory description on a signboard which says:

> *"Shennong Merit & Virtue Forest was established in the 1990s. Numerous outstanding people planted trees here to contribute to the greenness and to propagate merits and virtues. More than 2,000 individual plants including 40 ancient, rare and endangered species have been collected here, continuing the spirit of Shennong, the Red Emperor."*

Apparently Western botanists have helped to work on this forest for the past five decades, identifying and classifying various herbal plants, and defining their medicinal effects. I walked past wooden labels that showed the names of several medicinal plants including *Paeonia suffruticosa, Iris, Pachysandra terminalis, Coptis chinensis, Epimedium* and *Paeonia veitchii*, to name a few. On the same boards, the medicinal effects of these plants were described in the language of traditional Chinese medicine that is perhaps more comprehensible to the local residents in the mountains.

Fossil Rock

Next, I came face to face with a huge magnificent fossil rock made up of multiple layers. Many ferns were growing next to it. In front of the fossil was a plaque that carried a fascinating text:

> *"The Oldest Fossil. The Earth was born 4.6 billion years ago. At that time there was no life on Earth and the earliest known record of life is the organic carbon forming 4.1 billion years ago. About 3.7 billion years ago, stromatolites formed by microbial mats of microorganisms especially cyanobacter, also called cyanophyta algae, and the blue-green algae appeared. Cyanobacteria captured the carbonate from the sea water, then absorbed the particles of carbonate to form thin layers of carbonate. Year after year, the tiny blue-green algae continued absorbing carbonate and had grown into large stones like 'multi-layered steamed bread' called stromatolites – the oldest fossils."*

Upon reading the word "stromatolites" I suddenly realised that I was standing in front of something that represented an ancient visible lifeform.

Fossils are remnants of animal or plant life preserved in a sedimentary rock and are useful in the study of life and the evolutionary processes on earth. If anything, they are like a book that unravels the different shapes that life forms took to adapt to the changing environments in Earth's history. Stromatolites are supposedly the Earth's first visible-to-naked-eye lifeforms in the Precambrian period.[26]

[26] Precambrian period extends from about 4.6 billion years ago when the Earth was about to form to the beginning of the Cambrian period 541 million years ago when there was a sudden diversification of

Precambrian rocks therefore contain the oldest evidence of life. Apparently, the stromatolites disappeared from the ecosystem a billion years ago. This was similar to the dramatic extinction of the dinosaurs.

While I have read about stromatolites being found in places like Australia, Mexico and Brazil, this was the first time I was made aware of their presence in China. The blue-green algae mentioned on the plaque are primitive one-cell organisms. The fossils are characterised by alternating light and dark layers produced by trapping of sediment and limestone precipitation. For a moment, I felt as if I had travelled back in time to the ancient beginning of the Earth.

Thousand-Year-Old Tree

The primitive forest never fails to amaze me with wonders that are beyond my imagination.

As I continued with my stroll, I came face to face with a tree that has lived more than a thousand years. To me, this tree is like a "living fossil" as it has watched the rise and fall of many Chinese dynasties. A yarn of red cloth is wrapped around the tree trunk. A circular fence has been erected around the tree with a 2.5-metre radius. At the fence circumference are numerous bamboo sticks with yellow joss papers. The thought

---

multicellular life. The earliest life forms in the Precambrian period were represented by fossils that resemble algae, flagellates and stromatolites. The period is the earliest of the geologic ages and carries the bulk of the Earth's history. The layers of sedimentary rocks contain a permanent record of the Earth's past. The final stage of the period is thought to have been marked by a prolonged ice age. The Precambrian period is divided into two eons: Archean (4.6–2.5 billion years ago) and Proterozoic (2.5 billion to 541 million years ago). In Asia, rocks of the Archean age are known to be found in India, North China and the Yangtze region.

ran through my mind that this tree has survived many more centuries than even some strong kingdoms. I felt I needed some time to come to terms with a living object which is that old.

Aging and programmed cell death is a well-known process that occurs in most multicellular organisms and I wondered what was the secret behind some excessively long life–cycles in the plant kingdom? Research findings of scientists who have made comparative genetic studies between young and very old Gingko trees showed that the layer of cells behind the tree bark does not have a genetic programme for senescence or death. Hence, they are able to continue their programme for making immune defences even after hundreds of years.[27]

[27] "Multifeature analyses of vascular cambrial cells reveal longevity mechanisms in old Gingko biloba trees". Li Wang et al. https://www.pnas.org/content/early/2020/01/07/1916548117

Shennong Altar

Next I arrived at the Shennong Altar. The Altar is erected on a piece of flat land at the mountain top with slabs of floor tiles laid in accordance with the symbolism of the Five Elements in Chinese metaphysics – *metal, wood, water, fire* and *earth*. It is designed as a place for people to pay respect to the legendary emperor Shennong, who has contributed much to the botanical knowledge of herbal medicine in ancient China. There is a twin 200-step staircase leading upwards to the giant statue head of Shennong. There were pine-like trees lining both sides of the stairs, making the stairway look sacred. Interestingly, the statue head of Shennong was erected with two horns. Again, I stopped to contemplate the meaning.

Horns are traditionally regarded as a symbol of strength, power and supremacy. Man has had an emotional esteem for horned animals since time immemorial. Ancient gods and superbeings have horns. Witch doctors and medicine men of the West were also known to wear horned headdresses. In ancient Egypt the horn symbolises "what is above the head" and is understood as representing prestige and glory. In China, the nomads treasure their goats and cattle because they believe that their strengths are concentrated in their horns. In addition to their physical strength and power, many tribes regard the horns to symbolise spiritual strength as well.

Shennong Peak

I finally reached the mountain peak. I gave a sigh of relief. I saw a stone tablet stating that I was at an altitude of 3,106.2 metres above sea level and was a little taken aback. From my knowledge and personal experience, mountain sickness[28] would generally start to set in at altitudes typically 2,500 metres above sea level. Yet I was breathing seamlessly and comfortably.

Serious problems and complications with mountain sickness would commence with fluid starting to accumulate in the lungs, making a person feel breathless. Yet, I felt comfortable and well. This was despite the fact that I never took any prophylactic medication before the trip. I recalled a marked difference between this current experience and the symptoms of altitude sickness I felt on the Tibetan plateau some years ago when I was holidaying at a similar altitude.

[28] Mountain or altitude sickness is the effect of sudden exposure to low concentrations of oxygen in the air at high elevation. Symptoms include not only breathlessness, but dizziness, headache, vomiting and significant tiredness.

As I reflected on the possible reason, it came to my mind that the denominator of altitude sickness lies ultimately with the availability of oxygen. I then looked around at the mountain scenery and noted the vast amount of green forests. The answer became obvious. With the abundance of green vegetation that produces oxygen through photosynthesis, there was no lack of oxygen even at this level. Hence, the symptoms of altitude sickness would not arise.

Ape-Man

Nonetheless, with the high altitude in mind, I decided to slow down my walking pace. I took a stroll and shortly my attention was drawn to another poster that took me completely by surprise. It stated that the Ape-man had been sighted in this area by various local residents in the past!

With the mention of Ape-man, the term "missing link"[29] immediately came to mind. The term has led many of us to think that humans belong to the same family tree as all other animals and we are supposed to have a long-lost parent similar to the ape, whom we are still trying to discover. As far as I am aware, Ape-man is a term for primitive human ancestors, or so-called *hominids.* Darwin's theory of evolution generated the expectation that, somewhere in the fossil record, there should be evidence for a transitional form that was intermediate between the anthropoid apes and true human beings. The first such fossil that was in between apes and human was found by Eugene Dubois in 1893.

I then asked myself: "Am I supposed to anticipate the counterpart of the Yeti[30] in the Himalayas or the Bigfoot[31] of North America in this Eastern part of the world?"

Between legend and reality there have been many stories of man-like chimpanzees described and documented with poor-quality photographs. DNA analysis in recent times has shown that both human and chimpanzee genomes share a common ancestor, and the surmise is that they probably kept interbreeding for a long time after their genetic split. These stories have a great impact on Hollywood movies, and one that struck me most was the appearance of Yoda in *Star Wars.* I started to ask myself: "Did humanoids and primitive apes

---

[29] The term "missing link" was used to describe a hypothetical intermediate form in the evolution of antr

[30] *Yeti* is an ape-like creature taller than humans and is part of the history and folklore of the Himalayan people. It is largely regarded by the scientific community as legendary.

[31] *Bigfoot* is a strange ape-like figure that has supposedly been caught on camera and seen limbering on its hind legs. Most people regard the animal as fictitious although it has been described in written oral legends in Native American cultures.

interbreed? What exactly has been our ape-man relationship? Who exactly is our last common ancestor?"

I roamed for an hour on the mountain peak in deep contemplation. Having satisfied myself that, in this study trip, I had been lucky enough to gain first-hand experience of the evidence of evolution, I slowly began my mountain descent. I returned to my hotel room in a continuing state of meditative absorption.

Meditative Absorption

The word Oneness,
Means differently to different people,
It is a state of meditative absorption,
And meditative consciousness,
Where the mind becomes still,
And being totally aware of the present moment.

It is a process,
Of unifying oneself in body, mind and soul,
Where the body, mind and soul are aligned,
It is the eureka moment where everything is connected,
With the most important person you ever know,
Yourself, your true self.

In that moment nothing fazes you,
Nothing can be wrong,
When everything feels so right,
You are sturdy and strong,
You are soft and weak,
You are everything, and you are nothing.

The feeling of your presence is so strong,
That it overwhelms,
Yet, it's calm and peaceful,
A sense of security washes over you,
A single word forms on your lips, Oneness.
You are here, you are whole.

By: Chong Jia Yi

Chapter Six

Holistic Education

Our humanity is currently immersed in a rapidly changing socio-cultural environment. Many of us, as parents, are feeling that the conventional education being offered to our children today neither reflects our values nor heeds our views of who we feel we truly are. Many parents and teachers have begun asking how we can better prepare our children for successful adulthood in this day and age.

Undeniably, the school today is the main social institution in which most of us engage in formal, systematic learning. In most, if not all countries, the focus of our society is still on schools to prepare our children for adulthood. It is timely, therefore, to relook at our vision for modern education. We need to fit in with the changes in the 21st century. In line with the current trend towards mindfulness, we are being encouraged to consider the theoretic underpinnings of holistic education as part of our new learning philosophy.

Holism[32] is a way of conceiving individuals as wholesome beings. We have known for a long time that a whole system is always greater than the sum of its individual parts. Holistic education is based along the same lines of thinking. The ideology of being wholesome is constructed on the premise that each person finds

[32] Holism is a term that comes from Jan Christian Smut's book *Holism and Evolution*, 1926. It is derived from the concept of wholeness.

identity, meaning and purpose in life through his connections with the community, nature and spiritual values. It goes beyond the idea of knowledge-building through adding up the factual information acquired via the school curriculum.

The crux of holistic education is to nurture the development of the whole person and goes beyond intellectual training. It uses the wholesome approach to address the broadest development of the student at both the cognitive and affective levels. It aims to develop the student to the fullest and encourages him to be the very best and finest he can be. The approach enables him to experience all he can from life and attain his goals. The purpose is to prepare him for a fulfilling and productive life in which his skills and attributes are constantly being challenged.

As a broad concept, holistic education develops the individual's emotional, physical, social, artistic, creative and spiritual potential in a balanced and coordinated manner. This takes place at various levels.

At the *community* level, we want the student to be able to relate with other people to foster a sense of care. At the *society* level, the wholeness gives him a sense of control and encourages him to participate as a responsible citizen. This also encourages him to look at his environment at the level of the *planet*, in terms of ecological interdependence.

The defining aspect of holistic education ultimately lies with the *spiritual* level. This is because addressing spirituality in the curriculum reawakens the individual to a sense of awe and wonder and invokes a sense of connection to the universe. However, spirituality is not to be confused with the practice of religion. Religion is an institutionalised system of practices and attitudes that is grounded in the belief of a supernatural power based on the lives and teachings of a historical or archetypal figure. Spirituality, on the other hand, is our individual relationship with transcendent questions that confront us as human beings. It connotes an experience of connection with something larger than the self. Mahatma Gandhi succinctly described spirituality as that part of a person that cannot be separated from his thinking and actions and constitutes the morals and values that bring him joy. The holistic development of children is incomplete without spiritual development; to this end, spiritual values need to be cultivated.

Spiritual values are the integrative values of the human soul consisting of altruistic, humanistic, personal and affective values leading to the growth of personality. They include truthfulness, kindness, selflessness, steadfastness, humility, compassion, peace and, in particular, focus on the notion of wholeness. When someone says he is enjoying a state of wholeness or undivided *oneness*, it simply means that he is extremely happy or fulfilled.

Holistic Learning

A simplified way of understanding holistic learning is to perceive it as being the opposite of rote memorisation. Rote memorisation focuses on learning through individual compartments of information where every compartment is neatly organised and separated from each other like a computer filing system. Most schools have separate compartments for maths, physics, biology and chemistry. In biology, for instance, we have separate compartments for zoology and botany, and for chemistry we have further compartments in physical, organic and inorganic chemistry.

Unfortunately, the human brain does not work in the same way as a computer filing system. The brain is a network of interconnected nerve cells. When we need information, we are just hoping that we will stumble on the correct thread that will lead us to the correct compartment we want. Otherwise we find ourselves in trouble.

Holistic learning works differently from rote learning in that it does not keep subjects and concepts distinct. Rather, it interweaves subject matter together tightly by focusing on their interrelationships. In this way it opens up many neural paths to the concept that is created for learning. In the example in the previous chapter, a study visit to a nature reserve starts with observing a highway engineering design and connects it with environmental issues. It then connects knowledge of various natural herbs with botany and links the locality with history, ancient tribal culture, mythology, health and wellness. Interestingly, it also connects the nature reserve with geology and evolutionary theory pertaining to the origin of man and the Earth. It can be seen, therefore, that holistic learning is a form of learning through creating webs of information that link each other together.

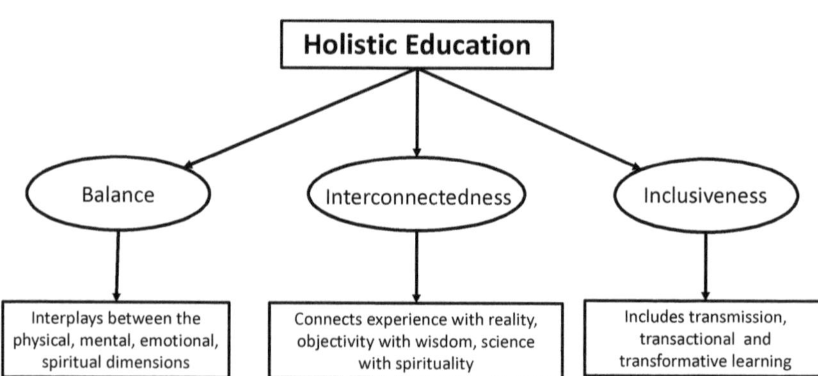

Holistic learning works with highly conceptualised information. The educational goal is to create a construct, an idea or a theory by bringing together various conceptual elements. This construct is formed from mental models. These models are built from bundles of information obtained through visceralisation, metaphors and exploring observations. By visceralisation, I am referring to the enhanced version of visualisation. When we visualise an object, we attempt to make mental pictures of it. When we visceralise we work to add other sensations, including sound, movements and feelings. It is analogous to the difference between watching a silent, black-and-white movie and watching the same movie in colour and with virtual reality.

The richness in holistic education is based on three principles – *interconnectedness, inclusiveness* and *balance.* These are in fact the same timeless principles of wholeness in human development. They embrace a number of personal, social and spiritual values and perceptions of what it means to be human in today's society and environment.

With the principle of *interconnectedness,* we move away from the fragmented approach in mainstream education. We avoid dividing students into various levels of learning abilities. Nor do we isolate the learning of content knowledge into different components and compartments. Instead, we aim to design a curriculum that emphasises the importance of connection at every level of learning. This enables the student to connect analytical with intuitive thinking, and to link himself as an individual with the community. He will then learn to integrate the body with the mind and the soul with the spirit more seamlessly.

The idea of interconnectedness provides a framework for the student to explore ways in which people, nature and objects interact to form a complex whole that operates as a single system. This sense of wholeness puts the student on a different platform. It helps him to see the impact of human-nature relationship on health. It also helps him to contextualise global concepts such as climate change and biodiversity. It puts him in real-world scenarios that he can understand. The focus of this approach is on the issue under inquiry rather than on the contribution of various discipline knowledge to answering the inquiry.

Inclusiveness refers to the embracing of all types of students, with a broad range of approaches to reach every type of learner. The student needs to learn about himself and he also needs to learn about relationships. He needs to learn to see the impact of social influence on his own self in relation to others. It is important that he learns about resilience, which entails overcoming difficulties, facing challenges and bouncing back from adversity. He also needs to learn to see the beauty of life and the world around him and to have awe and bliss in life.

The principle of *balance* refers to the recognition of complementary forces that need to be nurtured at every level of the universe. For example, rationality must be balanced with intuition in the learning process. Competition must be balanced with cooperation in the school environment. Ideas must be balanced with ideals in the area of personal growth. Individualism must be balanced with the greater social good. The concrete must be balanced with the abstract and, in this context, the emphasis of scientific thinking must be balanced with spirituality and value judgments.

We need to be mindful of how science and its mechanistic principles have contributed extensively to the creation of modern technology. We are researching deeply into artificial intelligence these days. Inevitably, such rapid technological growth can dampen certain human capacities. Many of us may not be aware that scientific thinking, on its own, lacks the mental capacities of intuition, wisdom, insight and appreciation for beauty. It drives us into seeing a person as a biological organism with a stimulus-response mechanism. We need to balance the outdoor learning environment with the indoor learning environment of classrooms, labs and computers. By developing the students' thinking processes and their connections with both indoor and outdoor environments, it offers them an opportunity to deal with scientific issues through their individual senses, thereby creating emotional experiences and insights that are not culture-dependent.

Today, the professional view of the nature of "human" is rapidly changing. Beyond objective approaches and concepts of measurable science, we realise that there is a lot in us that is non-mechanistic and not measurable. We are realising that the view of the mind as a computer is too limited. The practice of understanding phenomena by reducing them into component parts is slowly making way to complexity science,[33] in which behaviour is studied as a complex whole. We start to adopt the gestalt concept of the whole as being greater than the sum of its parts.

Contrary to our traditional way of thinking, the "more" is not derived from the "less" and we cannot understand "more" by looking at "less". To understand anything will require an understanding of its relationship to a larger whole. We must understand the whole in order to see the part. To be able to see the interconnectedness of all things with nature is now being recognised as the basis of the development of a new mind, the creation of which is the responsibility of education.

Our conventional education system is based on authoritarian classrooms. We believe that the designated authorities in content knowledge have all the answers

---

[33] Complexity science is the branch of knowledge that deals with complex systems and problems that are dynamic, unpredictable and multidimensional. It differs from the traditional cause-and-effect approach in that its thinking is non-linear.

with regards to learning how to assume responsibility, question what is right or wrong, and stand by our convictions. We believe that training our children and teenagers to obey rules unquestioningly and conform to codes of behaviour will achieve this end.

In holistic education, we take the view that the school should be a place where the relationships we want as adults must exist for the students as much as possible. In other words, we want open, honest and respectful communication where differences between people are appreciated. We recognise that interaction between people is based on mutual support rather than on competition and hierarchy. The classroom is seen as a community which lies within the larger community of the school. The school in turn is embedded in the larger community of the city or country, which in turn is embedded within the larger community of humanity.

The Mirror

With this holistic approach, people are able to find more fulfilment from nurturing and helping each other rather than competing to be placed above each other. The relationship between teachers and students is itself regarded as a source of education. This is because relationship functions as a mirror through which we see ourselves and how others respond to us. Everyone that we see around us is a mirror reflection of ourselves. The traits that we see clearly in them are often the traits that are strongest in ourselves.

Our relationships are in fact a great spiritual assignment in our lives. They provide an opportunity for us to experience our inner self and grow. Everything that we admire or dislike about others belongs to us. Our relationship with others provides a mirror image of what is going on within us. Through this image we get to know what beliefs we hold about love and life. Unconsciously we tend to be aligned with people who reflect back to us the areas we need to change in our lives. They also mirror back to us the space of self-love we have created for ourselves. As the student generates healthy relationships with his peers, he realises how these relationships can help to resolve many of his social and personal issues.

How Is Mindfulness Relevant?

Holistic educators see the sacredness in each individual student as something that they themselves should discover. This means that the teaching process goes beyond the imparting of knowledge to a process of discovery, unfolding and uncovering. The teacher's role changes to one that is less of an authority or sage and more of a friend, a facilitator and a mentor. Underlying all these is the need for the teacher to know himself better and improve his self-awareness. He needs to see himself in an objective way and avoid overestimating his virtuous qualities to boost self-esteem.

Knowing oneself is the core practice of mindfulness. There are many layers in self-awareness. When facing a group of students, the teacher who strives to be a better educator needs to ask himself several pertinent questions: "What is my experience with transmitting the content knowledge? What are my strengths that I can harness to guide my students to a better understanding of the subject matter?" Not every student learns and behaves the way the teacher expects. The teacher therefore needs to be mindful that he is committed to the fact that every learner has a compelling life story worth getting to know. He has a role therefore to help the student uncover how learning habits developed outside school may reflect on their learning ability in the classroom

Appreciating the role and importance of mindfulness in education requires us to be aware and appreciative of three areas: (a) educating the child means educating an entire nation; (b) in adapting to a rapidly changing world, the child must be capable of dealing with life as a whole; and (c) there are three layers of learning to help the child attain wholesomeness.

Traditional education is centred around *transmission learning.* This is based on the perspective that teaching is the act of supplying students with a designated body of knowledge in a predetermined order. In this regard, mindfulness practice is of paramount importance to help the student to cultivate the power of attention and focused concentration needed for transmission learning.

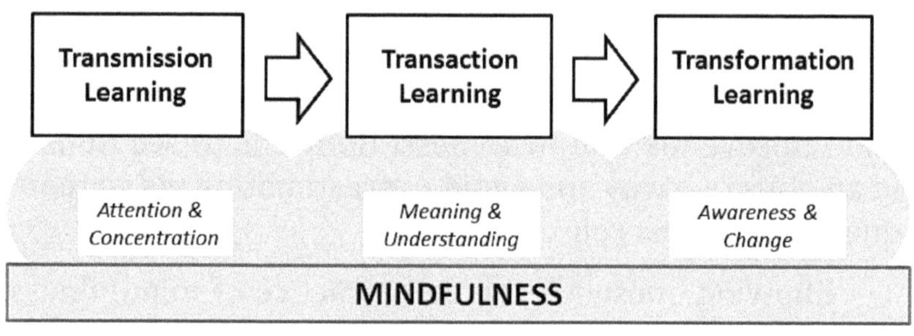

In a *transactional learning* environment, learning takes place through interaction with people and experiences. Increasingly, the philosophy of *constructivism* has penetrated many schools today. This takes the perspective that teaching should include the process of creating situations whereby the student is able to interact with the content to be learned in such a way that he is able to create new knowledge. In this approach, knowledge is not passively transmitted. Rather, it is actively built up by the student as he connects the new information with his own past knowledge and experiences. In this way the student is more able to use this newly created knowledge to solve real-world problems and come up with innovations that are valued in his social and cultural setting. This approach is based on the ability of the student to develop his own insights. Again, mindfulness practice is well recognised as a timeless tool to help the individual to cultivate meaning of concepts and generate insightful understanding of situations within a background of inner calm.

The focus of holistic education is always on wholeness. As highlighted earlier, the curriculum of holistic education is essentially a curriculum of connections. Holism focuses on the relationship between the whole and the part. Hence, teaching and learning approaches need to be rooted in a larger vision that includes a sense of connection. These approaches acknowledge that there is a part within us that is unknowable within the human psyche. The assumption is that we should nurture this special, or spiritual, part of our being to become whole. To this end, holistic education attempts to develop a teaching approach that is interconnected, dynamic and in harmony with the cosmos. Herein lies the basis of *transformation learning*.

In *transformation learning*, teaching is concerned with creating conditions that have the potential to transform the student on multiple levels, including their emotional, social, creative and spiritual dimensions. In this philosophy, learning is considered to have taken place when the student's experiences elicit a transformation of consciousness leading to a greater understanding of and care for self, community, environment and ultimately, the universe. It is through this process of becoming aware of his inner life that leads him to create a major change in his outer life.

Mindfulness is a major tool for self-transformation. It develops that part of our human nature which is constantly growing and moving towards a balanced and mature way of being. Our personality is determined not only by who we have been or what we have gone through, but also by the individual we strive to become. In transformation learning, the role of the teacher is to facilitate students towards self-actualisation. Self-actualisation is both the need and path to become what we have the potential to be. The school is a place for inquiry, where questions are considered equally as important as answers. It is also where the student develops a fuller knowledge and acceptance of his intrinsic nature. He then proceeds on a journey of actualising his capacities and talents towards the fulfilment of his personal life mission.

As human beings, we have a tendency to hold illusions because we do not know ourselves. To possess self-knowledge, we must first become free of illusions about ourselves and the people and world around us. Illusions consist of mistaken ideas we hold about ourselves. We make wrong assumptions as to our abilities and about our place and purpose in the world. It is difficult for most of us to break free from these illusions because they have become part of our habit patterns. Hence, we need mindfulness to free ourselves from illusion. To be able to change ourselves is the only way to gain self-knowledge and freedom.

Self-knowledge is fundamental to success in studies and career. A high school student who aspires to get into medical school may, upon self-reflection, realise that his fantasy of becoming a doctor has everything to do with living a certain lifestyle and nothing to do with treating physical illness. When he visualises the situation that, as a doctor, he will need to deal with very sick people and convey a sad diagnosis to their loved ones, he may find the prospects too anxiety-provoking. Dealing with issues of loss, disability and death may be simply too much responsibility for him to bear. Hence, he will understand that a medical career is unsuitable for him.

Mindfulness meditation is like a mirror to discover ourselves with our own eyes. Its use and purpose in the educational setting is to bring about changes to our own vulnerable self, improving what we see. The person who meditates realises that he is constantly creating his own reality. He understands that there are certain things in life that only need to be accepted, and that it is pointless to try to change the unchangeable.

We each have different talents and potential. Acceptance of who and what we are leads us to freedom and brings us to see new perspectives and opportunities. This expands the scope for creativity. Imagination and new strategies just flow, and the problem-solving process becomes much easier. We then see situations from a clear perspective. As a result, we become more confident and trusting of ourselves. We stop doubting ourselves, because deep down we know what needs to be done and learned. This leads to a simple feeling of joy. The unconscious mind plays a major role in controlling our life and behaviour, especially when we are not self-aware in the present moment.

The destination of all personal growth lies with the discovery and maturation of the inner self. The first step is to realise that our judgments and fears are created by ourselves. They capture our attention and keep us from focusing on the real blocks, which are our unconscious patterns. We hold on to the past and hide in the future. Doing so pacifies us and gives us a false sense of security. Gaining wholeness is dependent on breaking the patterns. Only then can new states of consciousness become possible.

We are always looking for the truth, even though it may be something that we don't realise. However, our view is always conditional upon the degree of awareness and responsibility we are adopting. The *higher self* is our inner essence as a person and the spiritual nature is our awareness and manifestation of higher values such as beauty, compassion, truth and love. Mindfulness meditation helps us to realise our own inner essence and integrate with our higher selves. With the harmony acquired we can be at rest within a storm.

The world whirls all around us in the field of our consciousness. The principle of insightful learning in mindfulness is how we manage the *Story of Self*. The "I" is both an observer and a participant in the centre of mindfulness. It is only at this centre that the observer is also the experiencer. At this centre he achieves freedom as he de-identifies himself from the controlling forces around him. Instead he achieves freedom and is able to master, direct and utilise these forces. Instead of being locked into fixed patterns, he can be in touch with unlimited potential for experience.

The practice of mindfulness helps us to cut off distractions from the unconscious mind and to experience the stillness centre. By increasing understanding, we are increasing awareness of truth, and are able to confront our lives with equanimity and take responsibility. All life experiences are part of our learning journey. When mistakes have been made, we need to learn from those mistakes. When we have learned the lesson that experience offers, we can then move on in pursuit of wholeness.

Wholeness

Picking up pieces with jagged edges,
As we grow, as we age,
Keeping each piece like it's a treasure,
Priceless and special,
A memory, a moment, a lesson.

We try to fit them together,
Fit them in boxes with a title outside
That is when we realise,
The edges don't fit and connect all the time,
And they still make sense.

Take a few steps back,
And look at them all,
As we grow,
As we age,
They are a whole.

When we have new pieces,
And we put them together,
It's still a whole,
With love they grow,
They fit and they connect.

By: Chong Jia Yi

Appendix I

A Mindfulness Script for Students

(This script is intended to be used as a guided meditation for beginners. It may be read out by the teacher to students in a class at a slow pace and in a low tone for optimal impact.)

Find a comfortable position on your chair and allow yourself to sit with your spine straight and your neck and shoulder relaxed. Put your hands on your lap and rest your feet firmly on your floor.

Close your eyes and let go of all your worries for the day. Slowly bring your attention to your sitting posture, exactly as you are. Just remain still. Feel a sense of being alert. At the same time be at ease with yourself. Slowly, let a feeling of relaxation dawn on you as you allow yourself and your thoughts to gradually float away.

Start by taking a deep breath. Breathe in gently through your nose. Then breathe out gently. Keep your breathing movement natural. Observe how your breathing is taking place. Focus your mind on your chest movement as you breathe in and out. Observe how the chest rises and falls as the air flows in and out of your body. Notice that your body knows exactly how much air it needs for each breath.

Continue to breathe normally and stay with your natural rhythm. Sit quietly and notice how your breaths are making you more focused and more alert. Next, bring your attention to the sensation of your breath at the nose.

Feel the sensation of the air flowing in through your nose. Let the air go down your throat into your lungs naturally. Then let it flow out of the body again through your nose naturally. After a few breaths, observe the difference in temperature of the air that is entering and leaving your nostrils. Be aware that with each breath cycle, you allow your outgoing breath to release the stress from your body and allow yourself to drift into deeper and deeper relaxation.

You don't have to do anything else. Just focus on the present moment and allow all your inner tension to be released with each breath. What you are doing at the present moment is all that matters. Allow your inner calmness to surface as you continue to observe each of your breaths.

Next, feel the relaxation over your scalp muscles. Allow the relaxation to come down slowly to your forehead and eyelids. Let the muscles of your face relax and allow your jaw to hang loosely. Gradually direct the flow of relaxation down to your neck and shoulder muscles.

Draw your attention to the sensation of your body sitting on your chair. Focus on the points of contact of your body with the chair. Notice for yourself whether the chair feels hard, firm or soft?

How do the muscles of your back and your buttocks feel? Are they soft, jumpy or sleepy? Feel the sense of the weight of your body on your chair. Let your hips and thighs relax. Now focus on your feet as they rest on the ground. Turn your attention to the pressure of the floor beneath your feet. Feel the pressure of your socks and shoes against the skin. What do your toes feel like? Are they warm, itchy or tingling in sensation?

Just stay at the present and continue to focus on your body. Anchor your awareness on your body sensations. Tune in your attention to how the sensations feel.

(pause)

Next, scan your body from head to toe and pick out the areas of tightness in the body. Allow the muscles of those areas to relax. Then send a wave of relaxation from the top of your head down, all the way to the tips of your toes.

At this stage, observe how your breath comes in and out like waves of the ocean. Is it fast? Is it slow? Or is it in between?

Next, you may find that your attention begins to wander. Various thoughts may appear. When this happens just say hello to your thoughts and then bring your attention back to your breathing.

If your mind starts to wander with thoughts about your studies, just bring your attention back to your breath. If you are thinking about meeting your peers and friends after class, just tell yourself that you have been distracted from your primary focus and gently bring your attention back to your breath. For now, breathing is all you have to observe and think about.

Let your thoughts pass by. Say hello to your thoughts and do not react to them. Just bring your awareness back to your breathing each time.

Now you may wish to focus on the feelings that arise within yourself. Take a look at the feeling that has surfaced. Are you feeling sad? Happy? Grumpy? Or are you filled with an eagerness to learn? Or to excel?

Notice that whatever feelings you are experiencing, be they positive or negative, can serve a useful purpose. It is alright to feel them. It is normal and natural to have feelings and emotions.

Slowly, when you are in tune to your body, you can allow your body and feelings to speak to you. Sense what your body is trying to tell you but stay neutral and do not react to it.

Picture the feeling of happiness within you. Where in your body is this feeling located? You can experience this feeling in this location now. Feel the sensations in your body that accompany your happiness. Allow the sensation to grow and feel the happiness expanding.

(pause)

When you are ready to conclude this process, keep with you this feeling of happiness and a feeling of calm. Notice the peacefulness your body is experiencing. You feel so safe and so very happy.

Now it is time to bring your awareness and attention back to the room you are sitting in. Notice the environment around you. Feel the chair you are sitting on. Is it soft or hard? Move your trunk, wriggle your fingers and stretch your shoulders.

When you are ready, slowly open your eyes and emerge.

Appendix II

A Mindfulness Programme for Schools and Universities

(This programme is contributed by a college teacher who uses the exercises below for students aged from 17 to 20.)

Introduction

School counsellors and teachers are frequently called upon to help students who face difficulty in coping with their emotions and schoolwork. Some students have underlying problems such as ADHD and mild autism or are distracted by traumatic experiences such as family break-ups. Others may face difficulty coping with their learning workload and meeting parental expectations. Such students need to regain their emotional stability and strength before rejoining their regular lessons to continue with the curriculum and catch up with the rest of the class. Under these circumstances, mindfulness is recognised as being an appropriate and powerful tool and is being increasingly used in combination with expressive art to enhance its healing potential.

For a long time, art has been used as a means of expression to help an individual make sense of the world around him. The culture he lives in would offer many clues as to how art could help to make sense of his social norms and communicate his values to other people.

In using expressive art for healing, the teacher or

parent needs to guide the student to create art in a manner so as to identify the issues residing within him. Intrinsic to our experience as humans is our quest to create meaning, and artmaking facilitates this process. Experience has shown that school children who have responded positively to mindfulness-based art therapy (MBAT)[34] are often those with anxiety disorders, anger and stress-related issues. This form of therapy applies the philosophy of mindfulness within the context of expressive art. In this setting, creative artmaking is useful for exploring the student's inner self.

Admittedly, art therapists are seldom available, and, in their absence, the teacher or parent may act as a substitute and learn the facilitation techniques to help the child. The mindfulness-based art programme described below is being used for older teenagers and adolescents. For younger children, the art activity can instead be simplified into a mindful colouring exercise. The latter is about consciously using colour and design to bring the child's awareness to the present moment. Instead of focusing on the breath as the meditative object as in a regular meditation, the child focuses on the weight of the colour pencil, the shade of the colour being used and his experience throughout the entire shading process. Materials such as crayons, paint, markers or oil pastels may all be used. The technique is a simple and effective way for the child to remain in control of his thoughts by focusing his mind on a relaxing task.

The process of applying the art materials to make a drawing or create an art image is known to have specific health benefits. These include psychological stability, calmness, focused attention, improved self-esteem, enhanced self-acceptance and better self-control, with an

---

[34] MBAT is an integration of mindfulness practice with making art therapeutically. The concept was introduced by psychologist Laury Rappaport in 2009.

ability to share one's inner thoughts. It helps the troubled teen to gain an understanding of himself, cope better and learn how to work through his socio-emotional problems.

Programme

The activities are conducted in two parts.

Session One: Safe Place Visualisation (10–15 minutes)

(a) Start with a breathing exercise. Take three deep breaths slowly with a focused attention on the individual's chest movements and the air flowing in and out of the chest.

(b) Let the student imagine that he is in a place he feels most happy and relaxed. It may be somewhere that he has been before, or a place that he dreams about. It can be a beach, a park, a garden or even his own bedroom. Tell him to take note of the scenery around him, the colour and shapes of the surroundings and his feelings of being in that place. Let him linger there for a while to enjoy the serenity.

(c) Ask the student to write down the experience of how he feels, both before and after the visualisation. Experience has shown that more than half the group would feedback that they feel relaxed and happy after the exercise. Many would even request for the exercise to be repeated.

Session Two: Mindful Art Creation (45–50 minutes)[35]

This consists of a mix of the following activities:

1. Expressive Art Exercise

---

[35] Teachers are encouraged to try these directives on themselves first. This is to help them familiarise themselves with any possible or unexpected reactions from the students, so they will be more prepared to deal with the pitfalls of carrying out such directives.

(a) Ask the students to make drawings of their moods and feelings. Do bear in mind that our lives, as humans, are full of complexities; and our thoughts, feelings, beliefs and experiences reflect these complexities. While experienced artists are capable of using art themes and colour tones to convey emotions, non-artistic students may have no idea of what to draw. For a start, simple examples may need to be quoted. For instance, if they feel happy, they can draw the sun, or if they feel sad or tumultuous within, they can draw a rainy or a stormy scene. The use of colours may help to reveal their moods. For instance, red indicates a strong emotion such as love and anger while yellow signifies optimism. Orange brings warmth, enthusiasm and joy; pink implies sensitivity; blue conveys calm and tranquility; and green is associated with a sense of refreshing, growth and abundance.

(b) Next, ask the students to write a letter to themselves as a form of reflection of who they are, how they are doing, and what they were feeling while creating the artwork. This is an opportunity for them to express themselves in writing, in addition to drawing. It is a powerful way of self-discovery. Sometimes the created art can resonate with the teacher and parent who are viewing it. It gives them an insight and identification of the expression that has previously been unrecognised. This is especially important when the created artwork acknowledges a difficult experience on the part of the child.

(c) Finally, instruct the students to line up in an open space. Ask them to close their eyes and respond to your questions by taking a step forward if the answer is *yes*, and remaining stationary if the answer is *no*. Examples of questions that are suitable would be: *Are you happy now? Do you enjoy coming to school? Can you sleep well at night? Do you feel stressed? Do you have a feeling of being left out? Do you feel that there are bullies in school? Do you feel good when you are inside the classroom? Are you feeling tired?*

Stress is a normal part of life and essential to the student's learning, growth and development. However, if the stress level is too high for too long, the environment becomes toxic and can be dangerous for health. This simple exercise is a good way for the teacher to identify students who are struggling to face their own challenges. In one case, the facilitating teacher was able, using this expressive art exercise, to identify depression in one female student. While expressing her feelings about herself during the exercise, she revealed suicidal thoughts and the teacher was alerted.

2. Collaborative Artmaking

(a) Divide up the class into groups of seven or eight students each. For each group ask the first student to take a piece of blank paper, write his name and what he wishes to see as the final art product (e.g. an ice-cream) on one side of the paper. Next, he flips to the opposite side of the paper and starts the artmaking process by drawing only one line as a prompt for the next student he passes the paper to. The receiving student, without looking at the back of the paper, is given two minutes to continue drawing from where the line ended. He is allowed to create any image he wishes. At the end of the two minutes, he passes his incomplete drawing to the third person. The process is then repeated for the remaining group participants. Soon the paper is filled up with an amalgamation of several persons' creation.

(b) Towards the end, the paper drawing goes back to the first student. He then compares what has appeared as the final art image with what he wishes to see. (In two instances, the teacher has witnessed a match. The student who wrote "ice cream" on the back saw, to his surprise, an ice-cream image being passed back to him; while another student who wrote "dying" identified an image of a coffin as part of the final artwork.)

As a cautionary note, it is not unusual for the teacher to encounter images that may appear worrisome, and they will need to handle the situation discreetly. If necessary, check with the student in private, on the intended meaning of the image generated. Avoid panicking or jumping to conclusions. While an image of a coffin may be a suicidal ideation for some people, it may well be simply an expression of "feeling stuck" in life for others, or perhaps a hangover from a horror movie viewed the night before. If needs be, the student may be referred to the school counsellor for further assessment or support.

Collaborative artmaking transcends the boundaries that normally divide people up as individuals. The exercise is based on our human desire for interaction and takes into account how students grow, mature and survive. This activity tends to work well with group members of approximately the same age and who are mentally in synch with each other. It has a value in developing strong relationships and healthy bonding.

3. Zentangle

The zentangle[36] is a method of drawing that involves geometric repetition. It is a useful tool for stress

---

[36] Zentangle was invented by a monk, Rick Roberts, and an artist, Maria Thomas, as a combination of meditation and art to help people who want to be creative but experience difficulty.
http://www.zentangle.com
http://m.golocalworcester.com/lifestyle/maria-thomas-and-rick-roberts-zentangles-a-worldwide-phenomenon/

reduction and frequently used in motivational training. The process itself is a ritual of creating a personal, unique and intimate environment. The goal is to promote calmness and a meditative state. It leverages on the individual's behaviour of refraining from planning so as to allow lines and shapes to emerge spontaneously during the artmaking process.

(a) Use a square piece of paper approximately 10 cm in side-length. Insert a pencil dot on each corner, about 0.6–0.8 cm away from the edge and join them up to form a square border. Inside the border draw pencil lines to make *strings*. Strings separate the tile into sections. The strings may be a series of straight lines going from one border to the next, or a curved line that touches the border now and again.

(b) Within the sections defined by the strings, draw tangles inside them. A *tangle* is a sequence of simple, repeated strokes that make up a pattern. Allow the mind to wander while drawing different patterns in each section. Erasers are not necessary. The process is random, and the student is not mentally attached to the outcome of his drawing. He can add strokes with a graphite pencil to bring contrast and dimension to the tile. Younger children may prefer to draw larger designs with felt pens. Upon completion, the student takes a step back to look at his tile and appreciate the patterns he has created.

Repetitive, creative work is itself calming and self-soothing. Every line in a zentangle is drawn consciously and thoughtfully, as if it is made up of thoughts and words. Zentangle is a simple way to calm an anxious mind, increase self-confidence and create moment-to-moment awareness. The process is relaxing, especially when there is no expected outcome. The student stays open to whatever pattern that emerges. In essence, the exercise is about connecting the mind with hand and paper, allowing thoughts and perspectives to flow out. Through the patterns, sizes, details and apparent tidiness of the drawings, the teacher may be able to pick up clues to the different characters within the class.

Appendix III

Mindfulness-based Art Expression

(The art exercises in this section are an in-depth extension of those in Appendix II and are generally more suited for older teens and young adults.)

Introduction

Our modern view of art has moved away from the concept of *imitation* to that of *expression*. Instead of seeing art as a reflection of the state of the external world, it is now perceived to reflect the inner world of the individual who created the art.

Increasingly, we recognise that the creative process is therapeutic in nature. Creative expression informs our feelings, actions and insights. The process of discovering ourselves through an artform coming from an emotional depth broadens our capacity to be mindful by adding insight to our inquiry. We are now aware that combining mindfulness and art expression helps to enhance the healing process.

The art exercises described here can be a fun way to bring additional mindfulness into our life. They can be used by the teacher in school or by the parent at home. The art materials required are basic, and include graphite pencils, crayons, colour markers, drawing paper, acrylic paint, brushes, palettes, coloured paper and glue. The approach encourages the student to develop art around a certain idea, such as how he sees himself and who he wants to become.

In all these exercises, the association with mindfulness is emphasised. Mindfulness provides the student with a mirror to see himself as a creator. This mindful observation of his own creative process facilitates the harvesting of meaning and insight from his artwork to apply to his life. The focus of the exercises is not so much on the final product, but more on facilitating the student to comment on his feelings or reactions to what he has created.

The teacher or parent who facilitates the creative process must refrain from interpreting the meaning underlying the created artwork. The whole idea is to leave the student to talk about whatever he chooses to share or what he feels is relevant about his artwork. The emphasis is on the creative process and he is encouraged to verbalise his thoughts and feelings upon completing his artwork. He needs to keep in mind that he is free from a sense of what his art product *should* look like. In particular, he must dissociate the way he views the art pieces in museums from the art he is creating to express himself.

Exercise 1: Drawing a Safe Place

Materials required: A few A4 sheets of paper; coloured pencils, water colours, acrylic paint or colour markers.

Theme: Feeling safe is a fundamental prerequisite for the healing process. The safe place may be looked upon as an emotional sanctuary into which a person can retreat in order to gain stability whenever he feels stressed. The safe-place visualisation is a useful therapeutic exercise to shape areas in one's inner world so that *going* to that safe place becomes almost natural during times of stress. The technique is frequently used in psychotherapy to help individuals to feel calmer. For adolescents who have gone through traumatic experiences in their childhood, this exercise would be particularly relevant. Teachers and parents need to be sensitive to the reality that such students require a lot of emotional support when they turn inwards to discover that their imagined safe place can be a resource for comfort.

Step (a): Start with a mindfulness exercise using the guided imagery script below. The student can be prompted to connect with a real place that he has actually been to before and where he felt safe. However, he can choose to go beyond this to create, by harnessing his imaginary power, a fantasy place associated with a sense of inner peace and safety.

Guided Imagery Script:

Close your eyes and get into a comfortable sitting position. Begin by taking a slow, deep breath. Relax your body and focus on the movements of your chest and belly as you breathe in and out. (pause)

Take a second, deep breath slowly and concentrate on the sensation of the air entering and leaving your chest. (pause)

Take a third deep breath. Breathe in slowly ... and then breathe out slowly, allowing the outgoing breath to bring you into a state of relaxation. (pause)

As you are feeling calmer and more relaxed, think of a place where you feel safe. This can be anywhere: your bedroom, a holiday cottage, or it can be somewhere outdoors like a garden, a park, a meadow, a beach, an island or a scenic mountain. It can also be somewhere you have actually been to and felt safe. (pause)

After you have chosen a place, start to visualise the details. What can you see there? What do you hear or smell? How warm or cool is the place? You have all the freedom in the world to choose what you want to create for this place.

(pause)

Notice the details of your surroundings. Observe the colour and hues. Take note of the ground. Is it covered with soil or sand? What do you feel beneath your feet? How does the air smell? Is it sweet and refreshing? Are there birds singing overhead? What other sounds do you hear? Are there sounds of running water? Is there a waterfall? Do you see waves? Do you feel if there is a breeze or wind? Slowly, and in your own time, capture all these details. (pause)

Take your time and feel the sense of calm and serenity of this safe place. As you become part of the place, you feel more relaxed and more at peace. Slowly, after you have observed this place in detail, bring yourself back to the here and now, knowing that you can return to your safe place any time you wish. When you are ready, open your eyes and you can begin your art exercise.

Example 1: The Cave with a Spring

"I keep having this picture in my head and now I recall that this scene actually used to appear in my head when I was living in my parents' house at about twelve years of age. There has been a time when I kept seeing myself in a cave with a spring, but at that time I did not see any tables. However, in the picture I have in my head now, there are two

tables and I always have my meal at that table where I have drawn a bowl of rice. I recall the feeling I had was that the spring water was very cooling. I always felt peaceful, calm and contented whenever I played by the spring. I felt safe too."

Step (b): Next, ask the student to use the provided art materials to draw an image of the safe place he has chosen. Use the visual and experiential aspects of artmaking to help him bring his feelings to life. Art allows for a non-verbal telling which makes the individual feels safer and more likely to share his experience thereafter. There are no limitations as to what makes a place safe for an individual, though the priority is that of physical safety. Encourage the student to generate a mix of imaginative ideas and think of the things in his life that gives him comfort or security. He can then add these things to his picture of the safe place.

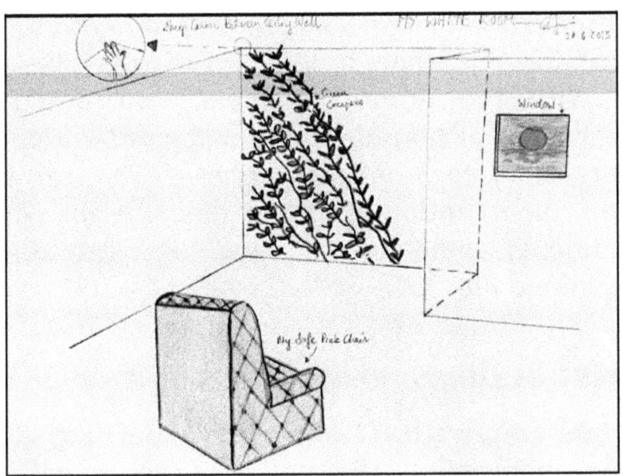

Example 2: My White Room

"I see my white room and my safe chair. I look through the window on the wall. It's sunset. The orange sun is setting against the seashore line. It's beautiful. I feel calm, relaxed and peaceful. It's quiet. The silence makes me feel peaceful. There is a pink hue in the room. I look out the window again,

the sky has since turned to a pink dusk. I like the serenity. I feel myself walking around the white room and touching the walls. They are glossy, shiny and smooth. I like the feeling and touch the walls all around. I feel good doing so. The room is cooling. I can feel my lip muscles tilted upwards into a smile. The window is very small, about two feet square. I like the room. I don't feel lonely in here but feel peaceful instead. There's a sharp corner in between every ceiling wall. I used my finger to poke at those corners. I keep poking because I feel so satisfied in doing so. It's like scoring a goal in a basketball game and seeing the ball fall into the net. I look out the window again. There is a boat with big sails. The wind is blowing against my long hair. I feel so peaceful. Again, I can feel myself smiling."

Step (c): Upon completion of the artwork, ask the student to take a mindful minute to reflect on what it was like to do the exercise. *How did he feel when he was creating the artwork? What did he notice about himself? What protective boundaries does he need to feel safe?* If he feels comfortable enough, ask him to share his created image with the group members, and describe the different parts of his safe space. *What is the significance and purpose of each of these features?* This can become the start of a continuing group dialogue on what safe environments could be and how to create something similar in real life.

Exercise 2: Discovering One's Self

Materials required: A4 sheets of paper; any available drawing materials including coloured pencils, water colours, acrylic paint and markers.

Theme: Most of us have been brought up to follow the rules of society and move with them. We spend the best years of our lives going to school to excel in academic performance. However, textbooks do not teach us anything about ourselves. Finding ourselves, and who we want to be, is really the most important adventure of our lives. Our journey of self-discovery may involve looking at our values, talents, passions, abilities and what inspires us. It is a never-ending journey that will help us to advance in every aspect of our lives. Through this exercise the student will learn to discover his own inner world of thoughts, imagination, desires and reflections. With self-discovery the student learns to accept himself and be less concerned about how others perceive him. It helps him to identify his difficulties, obstacles and issues he might have with his studies and relationships with his peers and teachers. He can also clarify the abilities that he possesses and can develop further.

Step (a): Start with a meditative exercise using the guided imagery script below, bearing in mind that self-discovery is about seeing clearly who we are. The integrated use of mindfulness meditation with art allows us to not only recognise the habits we already have but also identify other hidden capabilities and capacities.

Guided Imagery Script:

You are about to go on a guided imagery journey. Take a moment to ensure that you are seated in a comfortable position. Close your eyes. Take a deep breath and hold it for a moment. Then breathe out slowly. Allow any tension in your body to gradually fade away as you relax more deeply with the outgoing breath. (pause)

Take a second, deep breath. Breathe in slowly, focusing on the air entering your chest, and then breathe out slowly, concentrating on the air leaving your chest. (pause)

Take a third deep breath ... in slowly ... and out slowly. Allow the outgoing breath to help you drift into a state of deep relaxation, starting with the top of the head and flowing down to your neck. Let the relaxed sensation work its way down slowly, and deep into the muscles of your shoulders ... chest ... belly ... hips ... and all the way down to your thighs ... legs ... and feet. (pause)

You are now very relaxed, and it is time to embark on your journey of inner discovery. Imagine yourself walking down a busy street with lots of students hurrying to school. You make your way through the crowd, arrive at the school gate and step inside the entrance. You enter the school compound and now arrive at the top of a flight of stairs.

Slowly make your way down the stairs, step by step. As you do so, the noise of the school children begins to fade away. With each step you take down the stairs, you feel yourself moving away from the busy outside world. With every step you take, you also sink deeper and deeper into a state of peaceful relaxation. (pause)

You have now reached the bottom of the staircase and can barely hear the noise above you. You see a tall wooden door before you. Slowly, the door opens and you walk towards it. In front of you is a library. It is filled with books and shelves. You step inside the room and feel very safe and secure in this place.

In the centre of the room you see a small wooden desk. On the desk you notice a big dust-covered book. You feel a sense of wonder as you look at this grand old book. You step forward, open the book and notice that all the pages within are blank. You realise it is a book of freedom, and it has the power to free you from anything that is bothering you.

Think for a moment to find out what is troubling you in your school life. It is time now for you to write in the book any feelings that you are holding on to, anything that burdens you or holds you back. Imagine your achievements, thoughts and obstacles are being imprinted onto this book. You have a sense that the pages are slowly being filled up with all your concerns. As the pages fill up, you begin to feel lighter and more positive.

You now feel you have been heard and understood. Deep down, you hear your own voice speaking: "I am free to experience life the way I choose. I am free from all concerns about the past. My life and studies will unfold according to a perfect plan. I will simply allow the achievements I desire to flow to me. I am open to all of life's experiences. If and when problems arise, I will observe them with a calm and open mind, because I know they will all resolve with time. From now onward, my path forward is clear." (pause)

Now it is time for you to return to where you came from. You make your way back to the door. You walk through the door, step out of the library and make your way back to the stairs. You feel refreshed, clear and calm, and ready to come back to the here and now. Slowly, become aware of your body and the chair you are sitting on. When you are ready, open your eyes and find yourself back. You are now ready to begin your artwork.

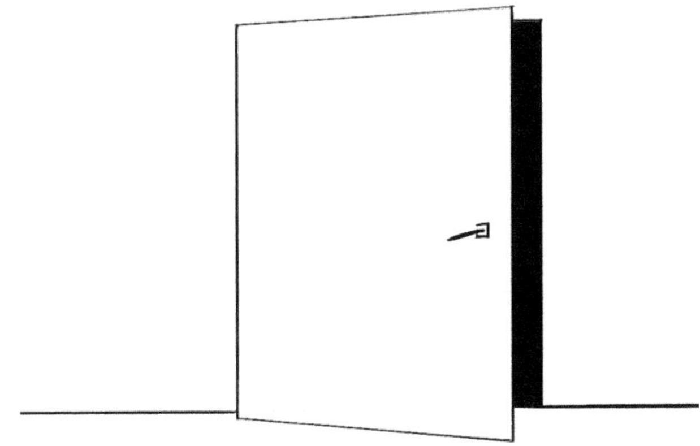

Step (b): Ask the student to draw a visual image of a door on one side of a piece of paper. The door is being used as a symbol of something that provokes curiosity and a metaphorical gateway to the future. However, the door can also represent an impediment to progress. Hence, after the student has sketched the image, ask him to write a couple of words on the door to represent his current reality, such as his achievements to date and the various obstacles and difficulties that get in his way. After writing each word, he may wish to add a small adjacent image to visually represent it, but it does not have to be precise. It can be just a question mark or an exclamation mark to symbolise an area of psychological tension.

Step (c): Next, let the student imagine that he is opening the door to step into his future. As he does so, he flips the paper over, and on the opposite page starts to draw an image of his desired future. This will probably represent a time when his studies will become less stressful and his life more peaceful. He has complete freedom over what he wishes to draw, and there is no right or wrong way of doing it.

In creating the image of the future, let him ask himself, what dream or vision does he want to turn into reality? How will he make it happen? He must first see a *picture* of that vision and believe in it before he can train his mind to execute that vision. With a picture, he will be able to visualise his future better. He is also free to choose the colours that represent the feeling attached to his future dream in filling up the image.

What is the boldest thing I can do to turn my vision into reality?

Upon completing the picture, he closes his eyes, mentally focuses on the picture and asks himself: *What is the most effective way to get there? What story do I want to tell myself about pursuing the particular path I have chosen?*

Generally, the stories we tell ourselves are accounts that feature ourselves in certain roles and describe our behaviour over long stretches of space and time. They tend to capture the attention of others in the group when shared. When carefully told, the stories externalise our imagination and illustrate the reward of properly considered behaviours. They also affirm our self-worth as someone who has wisdom to offer to others.

"Let me take a pause, be with nature and enjoy the view as the sun is setting. Although alone, the animals and plants are always there with me."

Step (d): As the artwork progresses, the student can take a step back and look at it from different angles. In essence, the story he tells about himself and how he views his place in the world are the things that make up his identity. He can add different colours and shapes to make it into a scene. He can also take the words of wisdom from somebody else and turn them into a drawing that is visually inspiring.

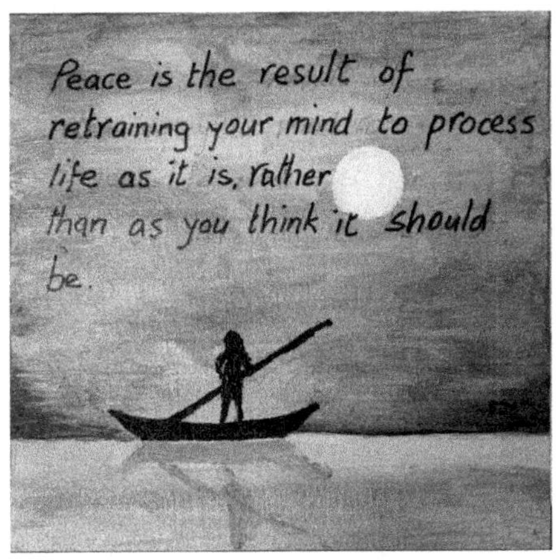

Exercise 3: Building Resilience

Materials required: A few A4 sheets of paper; any available drawing materials, including coloured pencils, water colours, acrylic paint or markers. For 3-D artwork the student may require, in addition, coloured cards, coloured tissue or crepe paper, glue, scissors, paper plates, coloured pipe cleaners and pompoms.

Theme: Resilience is about moving through difficult times and traumatic experiences, adapting oneself to them and keeping growing. It is something that can be learned. As parents and teachers, we can also help our students to cultivate it and strengthen themselves. The approach taken in this exercise is to move away from "fixing what's wrong" with the individual and instead "focus on what is right" with him through the use of a metaphor of resilience in nature.

Nature teaches us a lot about what it takes to survive in our world today. A tree branch that is laden with snow will bend under the weight of the snow and spring back to shape when the snow melts. Nature has built the same mechanism into us as human beings. The more self-aware we are, the better we understand where our strengths lie, and the more confident we are in our abilities to overcome life obstacles. When we are mindful, our ability to be self-aware improves and our capacity to reflect on our daily life is enhanced.

In this exercise we use the tree metaphor to illustrate different aspects of human growth. Upon the planting of a seed, roots develop, and the stem grows. The trunk gets taller and stronger and knows how to grow branches on its own. This is similar to how we, as humans, grow. We do not grow wild. Like the tree, we need to "prune" our goals at times to cut back on some parts to support others, so that in the end we will have more than what we are looking for. Through our network of roots, we learn from the soil environment about the availability of water and nutrition and the presence of diseases. The depth of penetration of our roots is also directly related to how resilient we can be.

Step (a): Place several photographs of nature on the table in front of the student group. These photos may include pictures of a plant growing in a gap between concrete slabs or of bamboo trees that are capable of bending but not breaking.

Start the exercise with a meditative session using the following mindfulness script.

Guided Imagery Script:

Begin by sitting comfortably on your chair and close your eyes. Find a position where you can relax and pay attention to your breathing. Take a deep breath and focus on the air entering your chest, and then on the air leaving your chest. (pause)

Take a second, deep breath ... focus on the air flowing in and then out of your body. Feel the energy flowing from the head down your body all the way to the toes. (pause)

Take a third deep breath slowly and allow the outgoing breath to bring you into deeper relaxation. (pause)

As you continue to drift deeper, imagine yourself sitting on soft feathery grass watching a beautiful sunset. As you sit there, you enjoy the stillness of the sky and the quiet solitude of the environment. This sense of solitude gives you the strength to be resilient in the face of your challenges. (pause)

Visualise a magnificent tree before you. Slowly walk towards it. Hear what it is whispering to you. Smell the fragrance and feel the texture of the tree. (pause)

Take another deep breath and allow yourself to merge into the centre of this tree. Imagine your body filling up the trunk. Feel your feet and legs sinking deep down and gradually into the ground to become a strong mesh of roots. In the meantime, visualise your arms, hands and fingers transforming into several strong and intricate branches while your head expands into the space among the foliage. (pause)

Observe the sprouting of leaves on your network of branches. You are now fully integrated into your tree with perfect stability. You can feel your flexibility as the tree sways in the wind, and your ability to bounce back each time. (pause)

Experience the life within you. The roots represent your strength and resources. The branches, leaves and fruits represent your achievements. Your achievements in turn indicate how you are able to face up to your challenges. Be aware of other trees around you and how you communicate with them. You have many lessons to share and stories to tell them.

Listen deeply within yourself. The tree has a personal message for you. Ask yourself: "What do I need to know with regards to building my resilience?" Take your time to reflect on the answer. (pause)

Now, withdraw your consciousness back from every part of the tree. Slowly, draw yourself out from its roots. Come out from the ground and return into your own body. When you are ready, slowly open your eyes. You may now begin your artwork.

Step (b): Instruct the student to recall his message from the tree and express it through his artwork, making a three-dimensional art model of the *tree of resilience* that he has visualised for himself. Alternatively, he can choose to draw a two-dimensional picture of the tree. The art product is intended to be a symbolic self-portrait that uses nature for inspiration. Encourage the student to thoughtfully attach a label on each of the bigger leaves with one idea that will help him to get through a difficult time. He may use keywords such as: *determination, deep breathing, music, friends, acceptance, ask for help*, etc.

3-D Artwork: Tree of Resilience

As the group members work on their art, conversations on their emerging products are likely to develop. When this happens, the time has come for each student to exteriorise his inner world. Assist them in processing their observations and experiences in the moment. For example, they may want to reflect on what success in life means to each of them.

2-D Artwork: Tree of Resilience

Step (c): When everyone has finished working on their art, let the group collectively view and talk about their work. The value of the exercise lies with witnessing each other's artwork while experiences are being shared. We all have stories to tell that prepare us in some way to be resilient and continue marching forwards.

We are part of a constantly unfolding narrative. Telling our story while being listened to with loving attention turns off our body's stress response and helps to heal our mind of anxiety, fear and the feeling of being disconnected from others. Sharing our stories is a step towards trusting ourselves, believing in our own inner strength and approaching our life journey with courage. Listening to something with an autobiographical context also has the ability to grip the attention of listeners emotionally and force them to rethink about themselves.

My Story: Confidence in my Strength and Abilities

"We have what we need. Just listen to our soul, follow our dream and live out our purpose of life. The force will be there with us. I am at a quarry. This is the first time I really climb with my hands, legs, butt; and grabbing the rocks, ropes, roots and tree trunk to move myself up and down."

Positive outlook, active coping, self-efficacy, and acceptance of limits and circumstances are some of the resilience skills that need to be developed. A key mechanism for developing resilience is finding meaning and purpose in one's life experiences. It is helpful therefore, to guide the student to reflect on his life purpose. *How would he use his gifts and talents to pursue an interest of his?* Let him go back to a time when he was able to overcome a major challenge in his life. *What did he do when the situation turned difficult? What personal strength did he draw on at that point in time?*

At the height of the Covid-19 coronavirus pandemic when this book is still being written, cities worldwide are being locked down in fear. Schools are closed for long periods and many students are facing the reality of having to graduate late. Social and safe distancing is promoted in nearly every country in the world. As a result, a tremendous strain is placed on the students as individuals, on their studies and on their relationships with family members. Many are facing a life-changing situation for the first time. This crisis provides an opportunity to reflect on how to make themselves, their families, communities and their nation more resilient. The student may wish to ask: *How might I endure long periods of forced isolation more effectively? How badly will my community be directly affected by the coronavirus? Will my friends and schoolmates get infected and risk death? When will I be able to resume classroom lessons?*

The unpredictability of the virus's behaviour, unknown duration of the global crisis and the realisation that everyone is equally vulnerable tend to shift our reflective thinking towards the existential level. *What message does the crisis have for me and for the entire human species? How do I prove my value as an individual without schooling? Who do I want to be when this pandemic is over? What is my mission to help the vulnerable? Which area of volunteer work would I be passionate in?*

Facing the challenge of a global adversity requires us to continually integrate ongoing lessons learned from the crisis. We may even want to re-evaluate our group identity with a focus on values and purpose. Most of all, we may wish to identify what matters most to us in life and what we should collectively be grateful for.

Bibliography

1. Bhikkhu Sujato, *A History of Mindfulness*, Santipada, 2012.
2. Howard Gardner, *Frames of Mind: The Theory of Multiple Intelligences*, Basic Books, 3rd ed, 2011.
3. Jon Kabat-Zinn, *Mindfulness Meditation for Everyday Life*, Piatkus Books, London, 2001.
4. Jon Kabat-Zinn, *Full Catastrophe Living: Using the Wisdom of Your Body and Mind to Face Stress, Pain and Illness*, Bantam, 2013.
5. Mark W. Muesse, *Practicing Mindfulness: An Introduction to Meditation*, Course Guidebook, The Great Courses, 2011.
6. Venerable Dhammasami, *Mindfulness Meditation Made Easy*, Inward Path, Penang, Malaysia, 1999.

About the Author

Dr Peter Mack graduated from the Faculty of Medicine of the University of Singapore. He specialises in surgery and holds Fellowships from the Royal College of Surgeons of Edinburgh, and the Royal College of Physicians and Surgeons of Glasgow, UK. He has a PhD in Medical Science from Lund University, Sweden; an MBA from the NUS Business School; a Master in Health Economics from Curtin University, Australia; and a Master in Medical Education from University of Dundee, UK. He is a certified hypnotherapist with NGH and IMDHA and holds a Diploma from the Past Life Regression Academy. He is the author of four books on healing and two books on teenage anxiety and depression.

Website: www.petermack.sg

Email: dr.pmack@gmail.com

Other Titles by the Author

Healing Deep Hurt Within

(English, Swedish, French and Spanish editions available)

Publisher: From the Heart Press, UK
Author: Dr Peter Mack

This book is based on a true story of an emotionally traumatised lady who suffered from unexplained syncope, dissociative amnesia, auditory hallucinations and suicidal tendencies. She recovered from her devasted state after intensive regression therapy over an 18-day period and moved on in life. Upon recovery she requested that her healing story be written up.

Life-Changing Moments in Inner Healing

Publisher: From the Heart Press, UK
Author: Dr Peter Mack

This book describes the healing stories in four individuals who had their problems resolved through regression therapy. The first story describes a person with unexplained visions of an unidentified lady; the second story is about a person who had to face problems of procrastination and anger management; the third had problems of memory loss and fear of success; while the fourth had a snake phobia.

Inner Healing Journey - A Medical Perspective

(English and Portuguese editions available)

Publisher: From the Heart Press, UK
Contributing Authors: Dr Peter Mack, Dr Soumya Rao, Dr Karin Maier-Henle, Dr Sergio Werner Bauer, Dr Moacir Oliveira, Dr Natwar Sharma

This book is co-written by six medical doctors from the International Society for Medical Advance and Research in Regression Therapy. It contains stories from eleven patients who underwent regression therapy for various issues including marriage crisis, inner child healing, self-love, refractory asthma, fibromyalgia, systemic lupus erythematosus and infertility. These story experiences came from four countries: Brazil, Germany, India and Singapore.

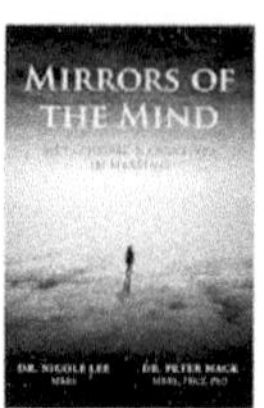

Mirrors of the Mind – Metaphoric Narratives in Healing

Publisher: From the Heart Press, UK
Contributing Authors: Dr Nicole Lee, Dr Peter Mack

This book describes the healing journey of a lady who experienced problems of victim mentality and buried anger. Her excursion into the subconscious mind brought forth remarkable meanings and insights into her symptoms and sadness. Her experiences, shared from both the patient and therapist perspectives, provide intriguing clues to the working of the inner psyche.

Bend Not Break – Learning from Loss

Publisher: Brahm Centre, Singapore
Author: Dr Peter Mack

This book describes the suicide story of a teenager who was unable to cope with the stress of his schoolwork and fragile romantic relationship. Included within is a discourse on resilience and the role of mindfulness meditation in helping the growing teenager to cope with emotional frailness.

You Are Not Alone: Understanding the Inner Voice of Depression in Young People

Publisher: Marshall Cavendish, Singapore
Author: Dr Peter Mack

This is a guide book for parents, teachers and caregivers and provides insight into the nature of adolescent anxiety and depression. It provides pointers as to how negative outcomes may be avoided. The book is written as an illumination of the inner dynamics of young people who are journeying through life challenges in a rapidly changing world of stressful situations.

www.ingramcontent.com/pod-product-compliance
Ingram Content Group UK Ltd.
Pitfield, Milton Keynes, MK11 3LW, UK
UKHW020419250726
13967UKWH00007B/2728

9 781999 923266